A String of Pearls

Vignettes of a Diplomat's Daughter

Chiquita Costen
with Joyce Miller

Publisher
Dallas, Texas

No portion of this material can be reproduced, copied, shared, recorded or otherwise manipulated or distributed without the written consent of the author or Dragonfly Press.

ISBN: 978-0-9854976-3-7

Copyright © 2025

In memory of my loving parents
Jule Benjamin Smith and Martha Ligon Smith

Contents

Dedication vii
Acknowledgements ix
Introduction xi

1. Last Flying Clipper from Europe 1
2. A String of Pearls 7
3. What's in a Name? 11
4. Assignment to Washington D.C 13
5. Prague, Czechoslovakia 15
6. Christmas in Old Warsaw – 1938 17
7. Escape from Poland 21
8. Wonderful Copenhagen 25
9. Stopover in Berlin 31
10. Barcelona 35
11. The Long Way Home 39
12. At Home in Fort Worth 45
13. Managua, Nicaragua 49
14. Return to Texas after Victory in Europe 65
15. Arrival in England on Victory over Japan Day 67
16. First Months in London 71
17. The Loveliness of Paris 73
18. Happy Days in England 75
19. On The Way to Budapest 79
20. Budapest: City of Romance, Mystery and Intrigue 81

21. School in Switzerland 89
22. Persona Non Grata 93
23. Christmas in Paris and Summer in Stockholm 95
24. Skiing Accident at Villars 97
25. Presentation at the Court of Saint James's........................... 99

Postscript...103
Ride! (previously published award-winning story)...................109
Historical References..113
About the Author 117

Dedication

This memoir is dedicated to the ones who matter most in my life and fill my heart with love and joy: my family. You are forever cherished.

George L. Foster, III
Jule Thomas Foster
Marian Minette Foster Frymire
Nicholas Edward Foster
Granddaughter: Caroline Elise Frymire and
her husband, Austen Baker White
Grandson: Benjamin Thomas Foster
Great-Grandson, Brooks Logan White
And to my young cousin, Patrick McGown

Acknowledgements

I wish to recognize and express my sincere appreciation to the Creative Writing and Literature Department of The Woman's Club of Fort Worth. It was in the Creative Writing Department where I first met these long-time friends.

    I wish to thank my good friend, Joyce Miller, current department chair, for her help in guiding the completion of this memoir and bringing it across the finish line. And many thanks to Dan Miller for putting up with us.

    I also wish to thank my long-time friends and fellow writers, Charlotte Tomlinson and Marian Haber, for their many hours of reviewing, proofing and editing the manuscript.

    A special acknowledgement also goes to my friend Marie Valden for her encouragement and support throughout this venture and to her team at Dragonfly Press for their contributions.

    Thank you, ladies!

Introduction

Many years ago my husband and I went to the Chautauqua Institute on Chautauqua Lake in southwestern New York State, for a series of lectures presented by four retired U.S. ambassadors.

The second day a lively petite ambassador stopped to speak with us. During the conversation I told her I was the daughter of an American diplomat and had spent most of my growing-up years in foreign posts. A big smile crossed her face and she impulsively hugged me as she called to the other ambassadors, "Guess what? We have a brat in our midst!" Brat, sometimes Diplobrat or FSB, is the name given to children of parents who serve full-time in Foreign Service posts.

They all wanted to talk to me over the next couple of days, and asked endless questions about my childhood and adolescent years abroad. They seemed fascinated by my stories of growing up in the diplomatic corps in the eventful years of the late 1930s and 1940s.

Before I left the conference the ambassadors insisted that I should write about my life. Now in my 90s I am doing just that – writing my story!

My name is Jule Martha Smith. My father was Jule Benjamin Smith, a career diplomat. Enclosed in these pages are a few of my memories.

Last Flying Clipper from Europe

In December of 1941, I am eight years old and living with my parents in Barcelona, Spain when we receive heart-breaking news; our family will be separated.

This devastating news comes in the form of an official letter my father receives from the U.S. Department of State. The State Department has issued an order: *All American citizens under the age of eighteen must return to the United States.*

My father, Jule Smith, is an American Diplomat assigned to the Consulate in Barcelona. Spain officially remains neutral, while everyone, including our government, watches and wonders if Francisco Franco, Spain's Fascist dictator, will embrace Nazism and join Germany and the Axis powers in the war that started in Europe on September 1, 1939 when Germany invaded Poland.

As the wife of a diplomat assigned to the American Consulate in Barcelona my mother, Martha, thinks she will be excluded from having to leave Europe. She is wrong. My father will remain at the American Consulate in Barcelona. Mother and I will return to the United States from Lisbon. She begins packing for the long trip home.

The day of departure arrives too soon. Mother and I both have tears in our eyes as we say good-bye to Daddy. He is close to crying too.

He hugs us again and again, tells us he loves us, asks us to be careful, and to take good care of each other.

Mother and I travel to Lisbon by train with instructions to contact the American Embassy. Portugal has remained neutral during the war and Lisbon is the only city in Europe where both the Allied and Axis powers openly operate. It has the most strategic harbor in Europe and has become a refuge for the multitudes of displaced people from all nations who want to leave Europe. It is the only hope of escape for tens of thousands of Europeans.

When we leave the train, we hire a car to take us to our hotel. The driver proceeds slowly through traffic and the throngs of people. We take in sights and sounds of this beautiful old city. The car windows are down and we hear babbling of many different languages.

Some pedestrians are stylish young women and men, probably natives of Lisbon, dressed in fashions reminiscent of Paris. There are uniformed military men from many different countries, both the Axis powers of Germany and Italy and the Allied powers of Great Britain and Canada. Many others on the streets are displaced refuges dressed in the traditional dress of their countries of origin. Some are Hasidic Jews, dressed in their distinctive religious clothing. I have heard that Lisbon is a city of spies and I imagine many of the men as villains, thieves, and assassins, although I know little of these types of characters. Many people on the streets look old and sick, some poorly dressed and dirty, and the men are unshaven. Pregnant women look like they don't feel well. I see people resting and sleeping on the sidewalks and in the parks. Some are curled up and sleeping in alleyways.

I draw closer to my mother as we ride through this maze of humanity. Before we reach the hotel she leans over, carefully watching my face as she admonishes me. "Chiquita, we must stay together at all times. We can't have any of your wondering off or exploring. If we get separated in this city we may never see each other again."

I am an adventuresome child, but the thought of losing my mother in this strange city terrifies me. I have no intention of leaving her, not for a second!

At the hotel we make our way to the registration desk. The hotel is elegant, but over-filled with people. We glance into the restaurant and the bars as we pass. Many of the people having lunch and drinks look rich and important. A friendly porter carries our luggage to our room which is spacious and comfortable. We are ready to relax after the long trip. We learn that a million refugees pass through the city's increasingly pricey hotels: the refugees who are fortunate to have money to pay.

The next morning we report to the United States Embassy. We are informed we will be leaving Lisbon on a Pan American Flying Clipper Ship within three or four days. In the meantime, we have instructions to report to the embassy daily in order to receive updates on our travel status.

The Pan American Flying Clippers are long range flying airplanes, designed to take-off and land in open seas. They were named after the famously fast clipper ships that sailed the seas in the 1860s.

The Clipper is the only commercial airliner capable of making regular flights over both the Atlantic and Pacific Oceans. And, it is the only airliner capable of making these trips in less than three or four days. Its initial flight from New York to Lisbon, which included a stop in the Azores, took only twenty-seven hours. During the war years the military modifies the Clipper to become a military transport, but the experienced Pan Am crews remain in charge.

For the next two weeks we are "bumped" from homeward bound flights in favor of higher priority passengers. While we wait for an available flight, Mother and I visit some of the sights of Lisbon, including the parks and statues, and go down to the harbor to watch the ships and crews. Ships of all nations are in the harbor including military ships of both sides. We also see various types of sailing craft, fishing boats, and commercial ships. As the days pass we become bolder with our exploring and take walks along the coast and on the beach.

Lisbon has the largest and finest Harbor in Europe. It is formed by the Tagus River, which rises in the mountains of Eastern Spain, flows westward, and empties into Lisbon harbor, an estuary where the mighty river meets ocean waters. From the harbor, the Tagus flows through a seven-mile strait, and pours into the Atlantic Ocean.

Finally Mother receives a call from the embassy. We are scheduled to leave Lisbon the next day. The embassy representative assures her we are fortunate to secure this flight. It will be the last commercial flying clipper to leave Lisbon.

The next morning Mother and I arrive at our designated meeting spot. This is my first air travel and I am excited. Dozens of other passengers mingle in the waiting area. I enjoy looking at the strange assortment of people traveling with us. Two of the diplomats are dressed in very formal clothes, medals included. They plan to arrive in New York the next day and present their credentials at the White House within five hours of landing. Another man who caught my eye has a briefcase chained to his wrist. We have previously traveled by train with a courier friend who kept his briefcase chained to this wrist, so I wasn't surprised. A couple with a pretty teen-aged, blonde-haired daughter caught my attention. An attractive, tall and thin lady, whom I learn is a well-known news correspondent, sat near us. There are only five women passengers on the flight.

Our clipper ship, designed for travel by the rich and originally very luxurious, has been modified for transport during wartime. Because I am the only child on board, the stewardesses arrange two of the extra jump seats into one larger seat so I can sleep more comfortably at night and take naps during the day. Our take-off from the Tagus River is on a grey, cloudy day and not much can be seen from the seaplane windows. We take off into the gloomy skies and climb through a solid overcast. Many cheers and shouts of "Ole!" come from the passengers when the plane finally breaks out of the clouds and into the sunshine.

At the age of eight, I have lived more than half of my lifetime in

Europe. I have lived in four different countries, speak five languages and been chased across half of the continent by Hitler's army, increasingly aware of the devastating effect the war is having on Europe and its peoples. Now I am among the fortunate ones, bound for America.

An adventure waits!

A String of Pearls

My parents, Jule Benjamin Smith Jr. and Martha Walker Ligon, are married in 1925 at the Episcopal Cathedral of Dallas, Texas, by the Bishop of the Dallas Diocese. My mother is twenty years of age. My father, a few years older, is around twenty-seven.

> *Doctor and Mrs. Robert Eugene Ligon,*
> *request the honour of your presence*
> *at the marriage of their daughter*
> *Martha Walker*
>
> *to*
>
> *Mr. Jule Benjamin Smith*
> *Saturday, the eighteenth February*
> *Nineteen hundred and twenty five*
> *at half after three o'clock*
> *Episcopal Cathedral of Dallas*
> *Dallas, Texas*
> *and afterward at the reception*

My parents created their first home in the neighboring city of Fort Worth and my father goes to work for his father in the family business. My grandfather, Jule Grey Smith, is a prominent businessman in the city. He owns Smith Brothers Grain Company and his brother runs

Bewley Mills, a familiar Fort Worth landmark. My father, an alumnus of the University of Texas and the Eastman School of Business in New York, has worked at Smith Brothers Grain since he was a teenager. His family expects him to someday take over the reins of the business.

After two years of working for Grandfather Smith, my father asks for a raise in salary. Grandfather Smith refuses. My father, familiar with the grain business, decides to find another job. Neither his uncle nor any of the businessmen and entrepreneurs he has known since childhood will hire him. Eventually, he discovers the reason why. The senior Jule Smith warns the small, close-knit business community of Fort Worth, "Don't hire my son." Grandfather Smith is a man who thinks he is always right; it is very likely, he thinks his actions will help his son "learn a good lesson" and return to the family business with humility and gratitude.

My father's riff with the elder Jule Smith causes him to consider his future in a whole new light. When his father-in-law, Dr. Ligon, hears the story he becomes indignant. "Well, I know some people, too!" The doctor contacts some friends in the Department of Commerce in Washington DC. Subsequently, the younger Jule Smith is offered a job by the United States Department of Commerce.

My parents discuss the decision together. They begin to reconsider his future in the Smith Brothers Grain Company under the authority of his father, while comparing it to a life of travel, maybe even adventure, with the Department of Commerce. He accepts the position.

My father's first assignment is in Buenos Aires, Argentina. From all accounts of this time period, my parents enjoy living in Buenos Aires and make many friends among the families of the diplomatic corps. My mother learns to speak Spanish fluently, a skill that serves her well throughout her years as the wife of an American diplomat.

During these first years in Argentina, my parents hope to welcome a baby into their home, but the years pass without having a child. They decide to try to adopt a baby in Buenos Aires and go through the required paperwork and interviews of an adoption agency.

One afternoon, after returning from her doctor's office for an annual check-up, my mother is sitting on her bed restringing a white pearl opera-length necklace. The phone rings and mother answers. It is the adoption agency informing her that they have a baby girl available for adoption and there are several other interested couples wanting to see her. My mother makes an appointment to visit the agency with my father the next day.

She returns to restringing her necklace, excited at the prospect of a possible adoption. The telephone rings again. This time it is her doctor's office calling to report her test results. She is pregnant! With an exclamation of joy, she drops the valuable pearls which scatter all over the floor leaving a white pearly trail into the next room.

What's in a Name?

I am born at German Hospital in Buenos Aires on July 13, 1933 and later christened in the Anglican Church by my Christian name, Jule Martha Smith.

My father wants to name the child, boy or girl, Jule. Mother wants to name a baby girl, Martha. My father agrees that if the baby is a girl, she can have a middle name of Martha, but he wants Jule for her first name.

In the hospital the nurses call me Chiquita, which in Spanish translates to "little girl" or "little one." At home my nurse continues to call me Chiquita and my parents soon join in this chorus. Chiquita is a widely used term of endearment in South American countries, traditionally only said to those very close to you, since it implies some degree of affection and intimacy. As native Texans, my parents think the name is "cute." The name follows me for the rest of my life.

My mother speaks Spanish to the household workers, community acquaintances, and to me as an infant. I learn Spanish and English simultaneously in those early years and my bilingual beginnings likely become the basis for my easy acquisition of foreign languages as my father's assignments take our family to several different countries.

When speaking directly to mother, I always call her Mamita, a term of endearment in Spanish, the equivalency to English speakers calling their mothers "mommy." I usually call my father by his first name, "Jule." So the Smiths become Chiquita, Mamita, and Jule -- nontraditional names for our small American family.

Assignment to Washington D.C.

Around the time I turn a year old, the Department of Commerce and the State Department merge part of their operations. My parents decide to join the State Department branch, thus beginning their life of moving every two years with a Diplobrat in tow.

My father's next assignment is to Washington D.C. He is granted several weeks of vacation between assignments and we return to Texas. We stay at the home of my paternal grandparents. The Smith Home, commissioned in 1918 by the senior Jule Smith, is a grand house on Fort Worth's beautiful, prestigious Elizabeth Boulevard.

Mother's father, Grandfather Ligon, is terminally ill in 1934 and in a tuberculosis sanitarium in Kerrville, Texas. For weeks, he has been expressing his deep, heartfelt wish to see "my baby daughter Martha and her little Chiquita" before he passes away. Mother is grateful for this time to spend with her father.

I don't have any memories of the time my family spent in Washington D.C. I am three years old when my father is assigned to Czechoslovakia. We leave Washington D.C. and take a train to New York City where we board the *SS America*. My first fleeting memories begin with vague remembrances of my parents, the transatlantic journey to Europe, and the train ride to Prague.

Prague, Czechoslovakia

I celebrate my fourth birthday that summer in Czechoslovakia and have a few scattered memories of the time we spend in Prague. I specifically remember living in a downstairs apartment with a garden, taking a walk after a lovely snowfall, enjoying the twinkling lights of the city in the whiteness of a winter evening, and receiving a special little gray lamb fur coat from my parents.

I have a child's garden set with a little rake, hoe and shovel and spend a lot of time playing in the large garden outside of our home. I particularly enjoy making daisy chains. Choose three daisy flowers with longer stems, braid them together, add more flowers and keep braiding until the chain is the desired length. *Learning to braid is my biggest challenge!*

The winter weather in Prague is terribly cold, often below freezing. It is dark by four in the afternoon and some days the light starts to fade by two.

It is difficult today to explain the importance of fur coats in countries like Czechoslovakia in the late 1930s. The long winters are frigid and fur garments such as fur lined coats, boots and hats are worn by everyone, both men and women, to protect them from the cold climate and wind chill. Only a few ladies and some men sport expensive fox, mink, sable, and chinchilla coats. Ordinary citizen wear cheaper pelts and second hand coats to protect them from the cold.

After moving to Prague, my mother buys a beautiful Persian lamb fur coat with a matching hat. I love to rub my hands over the fur and to snuggle into its folds when she wears it. Imagine my surprise and delight when my parents give me a gray lamb fur coat and matching hat. I adore the coat, love to wear it, and always feel very special when the coat and I draw accolades of admiration.

As a five year old child, I am protected and unaware of the war that is looming in Europe. The State Department knows the German invasion of Czechoslovakia is imminent and wants to get U.S. diplomats and their families out of the country. My father receives another assignment: Warsaw, Poland.

Christmas in Old Warsaw – 1938

In Warsaw we have an apartment on the second floor with a corner balcony overlooking a large park. The park frequently has entertainment with such attractions as puppet shows and carnivals. I love watching the people and activities from our balcony, and love spending time playing in the park with children from the neighborhood.

There is a long steep hill in the park and in the winter it is used for sledding. At the end of the hill is a coffee shop which is a cheerful gathering place for families. My parents often spend time at the coffee shop when I am sledding. At the end of my rides, I meet them there and enjoy some hot chocolate and a piece of chocolate candy.

It is Christmas Eve 1938 and I am sledding in the park across the street from our apartment. Mother tells me this will have to be my last ride before we go home for hot chocolate and dinner. From the top of the slope I can see bright lights shining from all the homes and buildings.

Christmas anticipation suddenly envelopes me like a white sparkly cloud descending on me as snowflakes fall gleaming in the twilight through the snow. The bright lights of the village homes and businesses shine through the large drifting flakes. It is a magical scene, made perfect for one five-year-old girl.

Bedtime is always right at seven. As long as Mother or Daddy read to me, I will drift right off to sleep. Tonight might be a little harder as I know Santa Claus will be coming to my house during the night and I desperately want to see him. I have often seen reindeer and always ask, "Are those Santa's?" only to be disappointed with the "no" answer.

Daddy arrives home just in time to read "The Night before Christmas" book to me. It is one of my favorites and I have lately begun to call my daddy, "Sugarplum." It always makes him smile. I struggle valiantly to stay awake, but the story soon has me asleep, dreaming of my own sugarplums.

The next morning I wake-up earlier than usual and remember it is Christmas. I jump out of bed and run down the hall to my parents' bedroom, hopping into their bed and bouncing, asking if Santa has come. Daddy opens one eye and gives me a kind of "grumble, grumble" response. Then he turns over and starts to tickle me. Mother sleeps through this early morning frivolity.

Daddy gets out of bed and takes my hand. "Let's go see and maybe Mamita will wake-up and manage some hot chocolate and cookies for us." We proceed down the hall as I gaily skip alongside of him trying to make him go faster by pulling at his arm. When we reach the end of the hall, the living room door is closed. Daddy stops and turns to me with a wink. "Shall we wait for Mamita?"

I jump up and down with excitement as I squeal, "No way!", an expression I have just learned.

Daddy slowly pulls the door open. The most beautiful Christmas tree I have ever seen glitters brilliantly in our living room. It touches the high ceiling of our apartment and the green of the tree is almost blotted out by being covered in bright lights, all the colors of the rainbow. The lights twinkle merrily making the tinsel sparkle. There are all sorts of presents under the tree, many of them almost hidden. Then I spy a beautiful red tricycle under the tree.

Each day I am usually a happy child and almost everything pleases me. Still I am overwhelmed by the beautiful sight before me. I squeal as I turn to my father. "Santa did come and he gave me exactly what I ask for!"

Mamita arrives and hugs me. She exclaims over the beauty of the tree as I excitedly run through the living room and hop on the tricycle. While waiting for breakfast and the opening of the presents, Daddy allows me to ride my new tricycle up and down the hallway.

Later in the day, our family goes to the park across from our apartment where there is a small carnival and other festivities in progress. On the sledding slope stands an enormous white bear, no doubt a neighbor in bear clothing, is bending down to push the children on their sleds down the long hill. He talks to the children and laughs and I decide he is a nice friendly bear. I am not afraid when he looms over me like a big tree before giving my sled a shove.

At the bottom of the hill where the snow piles up is a brightly lit gingerbread style coffee shop twinkling merrily through the snowflakes falling in the evening's twilight. As I warm up inside the shop, my parents come to get me. We go to the edge of the park for a sleigh ride in what I know is a *drotski*, a horse drawn sleigh. We bundle up in a red blanket to keep warm. After the sleigh ride, we go home and I tumble into bed. I tell Daddy it is the best day of my life.

That Christmas, celebrated in Warsaw, Poland so long ago, is the first Christmas I ever remember and the one Christmas I will never forget. It will be many years before I see bright lights in Europe again. Most of the continent will go dark after 1938; in almost all of the cities of Europe, nightly blackouts will replace the joys of festive lights.

Escape from Poland

During the summers of 1938 and 1939, several American families rent a house in Konstancin, a lovely resort village outside of Warsaw. It is a unique place, beautifully set in pine forests on the banks of the River Vistula.

There are seven of us children in the group and the rental agreement includes a cook and a maid. Each mother takes her turn as "house mother" for two weeks. She is usually joined on the weekends by her husband and other parents who travel from Warsaw by train.

Three of the children are my age and we have a wonderful time. One of my friends, Andrew Kostanecki, is a direct descendent of two American presidents, John Adams and John Quincy Adams. His American mother is married to a Polish Officer from Krakow, a pilot in the Polish Air Force.

Soon after celebrating my sixth birthday in July 1939, Mother and I travel to Lund, Sweden to have my tonsils and adenoids out. It is an adventure for me.

In spite of experiencing some discomfort in my throat, I am delighted to learn I can have ice cream anytime I ask for it. When I am released, we go directly to the vacation home in Konstancin.

We continue to enjoy the lovely summer as the threat of war looms across Europe. It is only a matter of time before Germany invades Poland. By Mid-August of 1939 my father is convinced the invasion is imminent. He and a friend, Mr. Strakes, an executive for an American cosmetic company, start planning to get their wives and three children out of Poland. They decide we should immediately leave for Norway.

We return to Warsaw to pack for the trip. Mother and I, along with the executive's wife and their two children, get into our car and start out to Holmenkollen, Norway, our refugee destination. Once out of Poland, the drive becomes a sightseeing adventure with stops in Latvia and Estonia. It is a week before we arrive at our destination in Holmenkollen.

The two families settle into a lovely hotel. Holmenkollen, a ski resort since the late 19th century, is both a mountain and a neighborhood overlooking the capitol city of Oslo. Ever since the end of the 1800s, Holmenkollen and the surrounding area have drawn large crowds of Norwegian ski enthusiasts every winter starting around the 1st part of December.

The families enjoy walks in the beautiful Holmenkollen area and excursions into Oslo. At our hotel we meet some royal princesses close to my age, Gabriella of Wurttemberg and Maria. They become our new playmates.

Days go by; there is no news from our fathers. Our mothers become increasingly worried about their husbands. Then, Hitler's army invades Poland. On September 1st the newspapers announce in gigantic headlines: *Nazi Germany Invades Poland*. The fighting is fierce and the death toll quickly rises. Our mothers listen to the radio broadcasts throughout the following days. By September 3rd the announcement comes that England and France have declared war against Germany.

Right after the news of these new declarations of war, our mothers receive news that their husbands are safe in Estonia. As the German Army blitzed into Poland from the west, the men drove north, crossing the border at midnight and continuing to Tallinn, Estonia. In a few days the families reunite and the Strakes soon depart from Holmenkollen. I am left with my parents and new playmates. Our family retains our refugee status in Norway for almost a month. By this time, it is impossible for my parents to completely protect me from the realities of this war. Even at six, I cannot escape the myriad of stories and rumors and become increasingly aware of the tensions sweeping across Europe. Newspaper images show civilian sufferings in Poland during the German invasion. Grim-faced adults huddle around radios that constantly broadcast news of the war. One country after another declares war and Europe is divided into the Allied and Axis powers. I learn my friend Andrew's father dies while fighting the Nazis in Poland.

In late September my father receives news of his next assignment: Copenhagen, Denmark.

Wonderful Copenhagen

In early-autumn of 1939, our family arrives in Copenhagen and settles into a lovely apartment in the city. At the outset of World War II in September 1939, Denmark declares its neutrality and joins with neither the Axis Powers nor the Allied Powers. During the first few months, life in Denmark remains relatively calm and safe amidst an uneasy peace.

A rapid succession of positive changes occurs for me. I am six and for the first time I will attend "real school." I am excited. The first couple of days, Mother walks to school with me to familiarize me with the route. Afterward, I am allowed to walk to school by myself, sometimes joining other students along the way.

On my first day of school, I find myself in a convent with black robed ladies who speak a foreign language that I am expected to learn. French! By the second day, I am beginning to catch on to what the teachers are telling us to do, thus beginning my life-long love of the French language. I have some "catching-up" to do as I arrive in Copenhagen a little after the fall semester begins. The nuns are helpful and kind so I advance quickly. I love being with so many children my own age.

I also join an after-school organization. In English the name translates as "Danish Children." It is roughly the equivalent of the American Camp Fire Girls organization. The other girls in the after-school program speak Danish and meetings are very interactive: playing together, learning new games and singing songs. Eager to make friends, I work hard to pick up some Danish words and phrases.

My best friend in Copenhagen is Elna, the daughter of the apartment manager. Elna speaks Danish and this is another incentive for me to learn the language.

Not long after starting school, I acquire a Governess, a Frau Larsen, who is a German lady living in Denmark. I instantly fall in love with her. Now I have someone to help me with my homework, play with me, and take me to fun places. Frau Larsen, like so many Europeans, speaks several languages. I learn that people like for you to speak to them in their language. I enjoy listening to her when she speaks German and try to acquire German language skills. Initially I pick up simple phrases like *'Guten Morgen,' 'Bitte'* and *'Danke.'* Frau Larsen is eager to help me learn German and I am a willing student. Sometimes, we will start out speaking in English, switch to French as we discuss school assignments, convert to Danish if Elna shows up, and end up conversing in German before bedtime.

One of the things I remember about living in Copenhagen is the nightly routine of getting ready for bed. The apartment has one small bathroom warmed by a large coal burning stove. The bathtub sets on four legs and, if full, would be too deep for me. I always accompany Frau Larsen to watch her stoking the fire until it starts getting hot. Then two large kettles are put on the stove to heat water for the tub. At that point I gather my pajamas, tell my parents good night and check that my homework is in place for the next morning. By then Frau Larsen has turned on the cold water to get the temperature "just right." She assists me into the tub, holds a towel up to the stove to warm it, and wraps it around me when I come out. By this time the bathroom is warm and toasty for my parents.

After I settle into bed a book is read or a story is told to me. An extremely active child, I am usually tired by bedtime and quickly fall asleep.

In the winter, I look forward to Saturday mornings because my father takes me ice skating. We go skating in the large nearby Langelinie Park. A statue of Hans Christian Anderson's "Little Mermaid" sits on a rock near the harbor. The ice rink is named the *Vanillian Ice* (Vanilla Ice). The rink is quite large and is surrounded by trees and a walking trail that goes all of the way around the rink. I am very proud of my tall handsome father and love to spend this special time with him. I love it when people tease me and ask if he is my older brother. He loves it too, as he is actually an "older" father.

Circumstances in Copenhagen begin to change as the possibility of a German invasion becomes more likely. The once lighted streets become dark. Black curtains are required to cover all of the windows, not even a slice of light is allowed to appear once darkness falls, which in the winter is around four o'clock in the afternoon. As weeks pass, we begin hearing airplanes firing hostile machine guns in the far distance and the sounds of Danish anti-aircraft guns returning fire. Then comes the night the air raid sirens start sounding and the apartment basement becomes a bomb shelter for residents.

At first, I am frightened to be awakened in the middle of the night and rushed down to the basement apartment. Soon I begin to see it as an adventure that happens at some time every night. Getting dressed is unnecessary. Everyone arrives in robes and slippers. Elna and I meet in a corner of the shelter and play together with our dolls until the "all clear" is sounded.

In the spring of 1940 my father receives notice of a new assignment: the American consulate in Barcelona, Spain. We are scheduled to depart for Barcelona by train on the morning of April 9th. We leave our apartment the night before and check into the hotel attached to the train station.

Early the next morning, I am awakened by a roaring noise in the distance. I look around. It is before dawn. I see my father silhouetted against the window looking up toward the sky. In a few moments, there seems to be hundreds of planes flying overhead. Daddy turns from the window, goes over to the bed and wakes my mother.

"Martha, the Germans are invading and their guards will be in place before anyone wakes up and realizes what has happened. I'm going to the British Embassy and hope I can get in." Mother is immediately alert, gets out of bed, and goes over to where he is hurriedly dressing. Seeing that I am awake she reassures me and whispers that I should go back to sleep. Being a child, I drift back into a peaceful slumber while my parents talk.

Daddy does get to the British Embassy where he is provided refuge and protection. Denmark does not have enough resources to defend itself against the powerful German Army and surrenders. The Germans subsequently declare my father to be under "house arrest."

The rules of diplomacy are complicated, especially to a young child. I struggle to understand what is happening. An embassy in a foreign country is considered on its own country's soil and under its own country's laws. The British Embassy has the authority to give my father sanctuary, but only within the walls of that embassy "house." Outside the embassy, he can be arrested and jailed without any reason at all.

The hotel attached to the train station is soon filled with high ranking German officers. Mother and I are having breakfast in the hotel and a German officer, a general field marshal, comes over to our table to talk to her. He is aware that my father has sought sanctuary at the British Embassy and assures her that she has "nothing to worry about." My father is safe and should soon be released from "house arrest." He points out that our two countries are not at war and we are not enemies. He expresses the hope that America will "stay out" of the war in Europe.

Mother and I make daily visits to the British Embassy. Mother brings Daddy an afternoon meal, and sometimes exchanges packages of clean clothes with ones he has worn. Of course the items are always examined by the German soldiers before they are given to him.

The handsome young German guards at the British Embassy are always friendly to me when I arrive at the embassy with my mother. I am fluent in German and enjoy talking to them. Soon they are greeting me by name. They like to tease me and I love the attention. This is a source of great consternation to Mother. She repeatedly warns me about all of the things I shouldn't say or tell them.

The first floor of the embassy is a half-basement. The second story window at which my father appears when we visit is only a half-story off the ground. By standing on mother's shoulders I am able to reach the window to hand him things like lunch and a change of underwear wrapped in brown paper. Conversation is difficult, but Daddy always seems happy to see us.

My father's confinement at the British Embassy lasts for two weeks. When he is released our family returns to our apartment, waiting for permission to leave Copenhagen and travel to Spain. Under German occupation many things in Denmark change. However, my life resumes much as it was before the occupation.

Although the skating season has ended, my father and I continue our Saturday outings to Langelinie Park. Nearly every Saturday I see an attractive lady pushing a large baby carriage in the park. I soon learn she is Crown Princess Ingrid of Denmark, the wife of Crown Prince Frederik (IX). The baby in the carriage is Princess Margrethe, the future Queen of Denmark, whose birth took place just one week after the beginning of Nazi Germany's invasion and occupation of Denmark.

Denmark's royalty in those days didn't have security guards when they went out among the citizenry of Copenhagen. Danish people love the whole royal family, especially King Christian X, the grandfather of little Princess Margrethe. The King walks among them as any business man would and always has time to talk to those who speak to him.

The first afternoon I see Princess Ingrid in the park, I go home and tell my mother how beautiful she is and how beautifully she dresses. I continue to tell my mother about the beautiful princess almost every Saturday. I describe her dresses as ball gowns, her hats as tiaras filled with jewels, and her shoes as colorful and elaborate dancing slippers that match her elegant gowns. Daddy always winks at mother and disappears when I begin my stories. Mother assures me that I am exaggerating my stories about the princess. I insist they are just as I remember her.

I celebrate my seventh birthday in Copenhagen on July 13, 1940. As I recall, permission to leave Denmark comes around early August.

Mother corresponds with Frau Larsen over the years. After the invasion of Denmark, Frau Larsen chooses to live with some relatives in the countryside. Because she has some Jewish ancestry she feels uncomfortable in the occupied city. After the war, Frau Larsen migrates to America.

Stopover in Berlin

On our way to Barcelona, my parents decide to stop in Berlin for a couple of days to visit friends. We stay downtown at the Adlon Hotel, one of the most famous hotels in Europe. The hotel and grounds are filled with workers in the process of building a long platform with a raised podium. A parade honoring the Hitler Youth Organization of the Nazi party (*Hitlerjugend*) is scheduled for the next day. I am excited at the prospect of seeing the marching boys in the parade.

Berlin is a beautiful city and has been spared from any fighting in the region or from any destruction due to bombings. We do a little sightseeing and enjoy walking down the wide boulevards past the beautiful parks and lakes. We walk down to the Brandenburg Gate, located right up the street from where we are staying. Afterward, we return to the hotel and I take a nap.

When I wake up my parents tell me we are going to a cocktail dinner party. Under the circumstances it is not unusual for me to accompany them to this adult event. Once again Mother reminds me to be seen, but not heard! I am the only child at the party and the other guests made me feel welcome by engaging me in conversation, complimenting my dress, and admiring my tight bouncy curls.

At exactly 8:50 we are directed into the library. The group, mostly Americans, squeezes in and at 9:00 o'clock a shortwave radio is turned on to the British Broadcasting Corporation. Listening to BBC

Radio is highly illegal in Germany and countries under their control. Immediately after the BBC program ends we all leave without further discussion.

It is past my bedtime when we return to our room and I go straight to bed. During the night, air raid sirens sound. My father wants to know what is going on, so he goes up to the roof where the anti-aircraft guns are positioned. Mother is tired and I am sleeping soundly so we don't go to the air raid shelter. I sleep peacefully through the first bombing of Berlin by the Royal Air Force. This night bombing by the RAF does not inflict much harm, but the iconic Brandenburg Gate suffers some damage.

The next morning the hotel is in chaos with the staff workers trying to clean up from the bombing. We have breakfast and go outside to wait for the Jugend Parade. I have never seen a military parade and it is exciting to look around at the flags and banners and cheering crowds.

Large tanks and other weapons of warfare pass by, hundreds of soldiers march with a special goose step performed during military parades and other ceremonies, large groups of marchers represent the younger youth groups ages ten to fourteen. The older girls, the League of German Girls, are also well represented in the parade. The parade's largest participating group is the Hitler Youth Organization for boys fourteen to eighteen. I am so impressed. I love the marching bands and the good looking young boys!

The crowds give thousands of Nazi salutes during the parade and cheers with shouts of "Heil Hitler" and "Sieg Heil!" As the parade ends, Hitler himself appears on the stage platform and the crowds go wild with Nazi salutes and cheering. He looks mad and immediately begins shouting and screaming and telling the crowd what he will do to London in retaliation for bombing Berlin. He raves and rants about the British swine that will soon be a part of the German Reich. He screeches that he will see to it that London is bombed until not one stone is left upright in the city. My parents remain quiet and their faces are serious. Hitler abruptly ends his speech and leaves immediately. The shouting and yelling of the crowds continue after he is gone.

Although I am fluent in conversational German, it is clear to me that the people are shouting obscenities and other words and phrases I don't understand. I ask my father and he tells me I don't need to understand those words.

Shortly thereafter, we resume our trip to Barcelona. We are happy to be leaving Germany after the bombing and unpleasant mood of the city.

Barcelona

We arrive in Barcelona and move into a lovely six story mansion that is being divided into several apartments. Our apartment has a large balcony from which we can look into the home and yard of our next door neighbor. The family has two teen age daughters who are making their social debuts and the event is to be held in their home. As we have just arrived and school is not yet in session, I watch the preparations and parties from my balcony which entertains me for several days.

Everything is so elegant. The attendees are gorgeous in their beautiful dresses, the music and dancing entertain me, and the fireworks displays in the backyard are spectacular. Every now and then one of the girls looks up at the balcony and waves at me. I wave back and feel like one of the party participants!

The owners of the mansion are building some new houses on their property across the street and offer to let our family move into one when it is finished. My parents accept their offer and help with the plans for our house. We end up with a lovely four bedroom home with a beautiful garden containing a square pond placed at the front entrance. The pond is fed by four ceramic frogs spewing water out of their mouths. I never tire of watching them.

Once again my mother enrolls me in a Catholic girls' school. I spoke Spanish as a young child living in Buenos Aires and this is helpful to me when settling into a school where Spanish is the primary language.

In those days it is a practice to have cigarettes and lighters for guests in the living area of your home. Cigarettes, like so many other things are rationed. People love coming to the home of an American and having the choice of popular American brands like Lucky Strike and Camels displayed on the coffee table.

One day a friend of mine and I decide to try smoking. (Remember, we are only seven or eight years old.) We decide the best place to try our smoking is on the steps leading into the gardens. We do this a few times over the next couple of months. One day my mother realizes cigarettes are disappearing and questions the help. Of course, at that point they give us up. My mother quickly puts a stop to our delinquency. I'm sure Mother devises some punishment for me, although I can't remember any specifics.

Our home sits at the bottom of Avenida Tibidabo and a funicular railway runs up our street to the top of Mount Tibidabo. There sits a tiny village with shops, a cathedral, and an amusement park. On clear days, the view is spectacular. You can see all the way to the ocean and most of Barcelona. I particularly like going up there on cloudy days, because the train goes right through the clouds and it is usually sunny at the amusement park.

I celebrate my eighth birthday in Barcelona in July of 1941. School resumes in the fall and we settle into a comfortable routine. The United States of America has not joined the war raging in Europe and Spain has remained neutral. Then everything changes.

On the morning of December 7, 1941, Japanese planes bomb Pearl Harbor, a naval base in the U.S. territory of Hawaii. They also attack other Asian-Pacific territories of the United States and the British Empire. Hawaiian time is eleven hours behind Barcelona and my father learns of the attacks by a call from the embassy in the late evening.

For the next few days my parents listen to the radio constantly for news updates. The day after the bombing of Pearl Harbor, the United States declares war on Japan. Then country after country declare war on other countries and join either the Allied or Axis powers. I am only eight years old but, having lived under German occupation in Denmark, I know the war is no longer a war in Europe. The whole world is at war and this includes my country, the United States of America.

My father receives a notice from the U.S. State Department. All Americans under the age of eighteen are required to leave Europe. I must return to the United States.

Mother packs for the long trip. We say tearful goodbyes to my father who remains at the American Consulate in Barcelona. Our destination is Lisbon, Portugal from where we will be transported back to the United States. After two weeks of anxious waiting in Lisbon, we secure passage on the last Pan Am Clipper ship leaving Europe.

The next day the Flying Clipper takes off from the waters of Lisbon Harbor. Based on information from embassy personnel, the airliner will take the southern route to avoid conflicts in the northern Atlantic. The passengers expect to be landing in New York Harbor in 27 hours with one stop for refueling during the transatlantic flight. For reasons that are never explained, the airliner takes a lengthy, circuitous route home, with take-offs and landings on four different continents. By the time the passengers of this flight land at the LaGuardia port two weeks later, the radio broadcasts and newspaper headlines across the world are tracking the mysterious route of this *Last Flying Clipper from Europe*.

The Long Way Home

Before daylight, the passengers are awakened by the stewardess' voice over the loud speaker announcing a change in plans. Instead of stopping in the Azores, we will land in Dakar, capital city of Senegal, Africa. It seems the airplane and crew has been recalled for a different mission.

After landing in Dakar the passengers are taken to a radio station housed in a hotel of sorts, definitely "of sorts." We enter a two-story gray concrete block building with miniscule sleeping rooms for workers who rotate in and out every two weeks. These will now be our sleeping quarters.

Dakar is on the equator and is hotter than Hades. Rooms are assigned and they are even hotter than the city. Everyone flees out of them quickly. Mother and I decide to explore the nearby area. Down the road lies a typical Senegal village. I am mesmerized looking at round houses with thatched roofs placed in a circle around the precious village well. The bare breasted women have babies on their hips and baskets of goods atop their heads. Mother gives me "that look." I'm to act as if seeing women's bare breasts is an everyday occurrence in my life.

Mother and I return to our hotel. The rooms have fans, but they offer little relief from the 104 degree heat and high humidity.

I am delighted to find the attractive American woman I noticed on the plane is assigned as our roommate. Her name is Inez Robb and she is delightful. I later find out that she is a nationally syndicated columnist for a big New York City newspaper. She is currently working as a war correspondent and is a celebrity in the journalistic world. The only other women on the flight are a blonde teen-age girl and her mother who are traveling with the girl's father, a diplomat.

The rooms in the hotel don't have private baths, only communal baths at the end of each hall. By bedtime Mother and Inez are down to their undies and their robes are packed away. Inez, a sort of "take charge" person, decides we will share my pink wool gabardine robe for trips to the bathroom. At seven years of age, I am pretty short. Mother is 5'2" and Inez is around 5'10". Fortunately my robe is floor length on me. It looks well enough on my mother, but on Inez it hits well above her knees. After she puts in on, she twirls around to model for us, and then sweeps out of the door and patters down the hall to the common lavatory.

The following day again looms hot and muggy. Grumbling and complaints by our fellow passengers are nonstop. It is an insult that they find themselves abandoned in this "God forsaken place." Then, the distinguished diplomats begin to remove their clothing. The strip tease starts with their coats, and then their ties and vests. Shirts are shed next and soon they are running around in their undershirts and slacks. Anything to avoid this dreadful heat! The diplomats appear to be self-conscious at first. Mother and Inez seem secretly amused. However, the mood improves among the passengers as we begin to recognize we are all in the same flying boat together.

During our time in Dakar, Inez buys a large ornamental gourd from one of the native women in the village market and presents it to me. I am so proud of my souvenir. Throughout the rest of the trip I carry it with me everywhere I go.

Within a few days the Flying Clipper returns to pick us up and finds a most bedraggled group of passengers. The passengers ask questions about the mission, of course, but "mum's the word." Apparently this has been labeled a secret mission and it is going to stay that way!

We continue the trip and our next stops are in Brazil. We land first at Natal and then fly on to Belem, Brazil where we spend a couple of nights while the airliner is on another "secret mission." Belem is located at the headwaters of the Amazon River. The first morning we make a hot and steamy trip down the river on a large ferry. The banks of the river are covered with heavy vegetation. Many of the passengers stay up on deck. Some of the passengers go into the large canteen area to read, play cards and have some drinks.

One of the guides on the ferry boat points out groups of fish called piranhas and gives a short lecture on these flesh eaters with their strong jaws and sharp teeth. Afterward, I worry about falling into the river and being eaten by these ferocious fish. The danger of these fish may be exaggerated, but those piranhas linger in my mind for a long time!

From Brazil we go to Trinidad and then to Bermuda to refuel. We spend the night in Bermuda. By the time we arrive, we are a motley group.

The weather in Bermuda is pleasant and a welcome change. We are taken to a very nice hotel to spend the night. The staff of the hotel greets us with a certain disdain, obviously perceiving us as a disreputable bunch. Too exhausted to worry about their low opinion, we are grateful to go to bed early and to slip between clean cool sheets.

The next morning the attitude of the staff is friendly and courteous. Maybe word has come to them that we are actually a group of important people being flown to the United States on the last Flying Clipper to leave Europe in World War II. The hotel prepares a scrumptious breakfast for us in a private dining room. The ladies are groomed and wear professional looking suits in anticipation of our arrival in New York. Showered, shaved and dressed in business attire, the men resume an air of propriety. The motley group is gone. Departure for the flight to New York is set for 2:00 in the afternoon.

The hotel manager arranges for a swarm of vendors to come after breakfast and show their wares before we departed for New York. Since

Bermuda is a free port, one doesn't pay taxes on goods purchased there. I gasp at the array of gorgeous cashmere sweaters in luscious colors. In those days cashmere clothing was a luxurious commodity.

While the women were trying on sweaters, the men became busy purchasing perfume and liquor as well as sweaters. I carry the decorative gourd Inez Robb purchased in Dakar with me during the entire trip. Now she presents me with another present, a pretty gold broach.

While we were shopping, a disagreement breaks out between the blonde teen-age girl and her father. She wants to purchase a cashmere sweater set. The emphasis is on *set*, the latest fashion fad. Her father insists she can buy only one sweater. She proceeds to go into the dressing room and a few minutes later, returns wearing a lovely blue sweater *set*. Her father again says, "No." I have to admit I want her to have both of the sweaters. She goes back into the dressing room and returns with a box containing the two sweaters. She apologizes sweetly and most abjectly and says, "Daddy dear, the strangest thing happened. While taking off the sweaters, I'm afraid I accidentally smeared them both with lipstick. I'm so sorry, but you see the vendor won't take them back." Her father is obviously embarrassed by this scene. He glares at her, lets out an exasperated sign, and buys the two sweaters. I must admit I rather admire her in that moment. She knows what she wants and goes after it "by hook or by crook" as the saying goes.

Hallelujah! The next day, the Clipper finally arrives in New York City and lands on Bowery Bay near LaGuardia Field's seaplane base. It is met by boats that tow it to the marina's terminal. When the passengers alight from the plane many of them, including my mother, have tears in their eyes.

Our arrival is on or around February 12, 1942 and we land during a winter storm. It is wonderful to feel the cold air and snow on my face!

The airport abounds with reporters and photographers, flashbulbs popping all over the place! Unbeknown to us passengers, our flight from Lisbon to New York City creates news all over the globe and the newspapers are chronicling our long flight home.

A String of Pearls

Our war correspondent, Inez Robb is a household name in the 1940s, and her newspaper, the *New York Times*, has been trying to discover the reason this 27 hour flight took two weeks to arrive in New York. Still carrying my ornamental gourd, I have my picture taken with Inez and am thrilled to see that picture on the front page of the *New York Times* the following day.

At the terminal all of the passengers say "good-bye" to one another, shaking hands or hugging and feeling grateful for landing safely on U.S. soil. Mother and I keep in close touch with Inez over the years and, of course, we never forget that dangerous seaplane ride in the midst of a war.

At Home in Fort Worth

Mother and I travel from New York City to Fort Worth, Texas. We move into the home of my paternal grandparents, the home commissioned in 1918 for my grandfather, Jule Smith. The mansion is on the beautiful street named Elizabeth Boulevard, a grand residential street of homes built for Texas oil, grain, and cattlemen in the early 1900s.

We were out of the country when Grandfather Smith passed away. Grandmother Smith has remained a widow. She seems pleased to have us in her home and makes us feel welcome. One of my aunts, a divorcee who lost her daughter, her only child, lives in the mansion with her.

In Barcelona, of course, I attended a Catholic girls' school. The teachers were nuns, and the classes were taught in Spanish. In Fort Worth I attend the local neighborhood school close to my Grandmother's home, Daggett Elementary School. I enjoy attending Daggett and roller skate to school and back home most of the time. I find classes taught in English to be a pleasant change and enjoy a lot of freedom playing with other children in the neighborhood.

This is the first year that Spanish is taught in the elementary schools of Fort Worth. When I return home the first day I complain to my mother about the class. "The Spanish teacher speaks terrible Spanish and tries to get everyone to pronounce the words wrong. She can't even pronounce *naranja*!" (Naranja translates to "orange" in

English). Mother admonishes me to keep quiet in class, do as I am told, and never ever to criticize the teacher's Spanish.

I love living in the mansion on Elizabeth Boulevard. Grandmother Smith is a gracious lady and I become fond of her. She gives a large party in July 1942 to celebrate my ninth birthday. It is held at her home. My school and neighborhood friends and cousins are all invited. The extended family of aunts and uncles and family friends are also invited so there is a crowd of happy birthday wishers and stacks of presents. The mansion and lawn are beautifully decorated and the party is festive. Tables and chairs fill the outside patio. Everyone seems to have a good time, Grandmother Smith included. When I thank her, she seems pleased with the success of the event.

Although Grandmother Smith appears well at the time of my birthday party, she is diagnosed with cancer and given only weeks to live. The rest of the summer Mother is busy taking care of her medical needs, trying to keep her comfortable, and helping to manage financial and household duties. Sadly, my grandmother passes away at the end of the summer.

With the passing of Grandmother Smith, Mother decides to go to New York and try to make arrangements to rejoin my father in Spain. She arranges for me to be a border at the large Catholic girls' school in Fort Worth, Our Lady of Victory Academy. The academy was founded by the Sisters of Saint Mary of Namur in 1910 as a day school and boarding school for young women and girls.

I have never been away from my mother, nor have I lived with other girls in a dormitory situation. At first I feel overwhelmed with so many changes coming so quickly. I worry about being away from both of my parents. Fortunately, the nuns at Our Lady of Victory are kind and I like every one of them. And, I enjoy being around so many girls my own age. I still miss my mother, but I absolutely love the school, the teachers and my classmates.

One memory I have of my time at Our Lady of Victory Academy is taking piano lessons and practicing on the student piano at the back of

Managua, Nicaragua

We move into a lovely home in a hillside suburb of Managua. The home has an open, airy plan. Our bedrooms surround a large patio with fountains and lots of beautiful flowers. There are no windows or other barriers between the rooms and the patios. When you enter the house, the living room is on the right and the dining room on the left. Farther down the hall, toward the back of the house, is where the servants live. They carry out cooking tasks under a tent-like structure outside of the servants' quarters.

My bedroom window overlooks this area where the servants prepare our meals. At first I enjoy calling down to the maids and asking for them to bring up ice cream, glasses of milk and other refreshments. It is fun until Mother catches me in the act. She tells the maids are not to wait on me as I am capable of getting these things myself.

In 1943 the schools in Nicaragua are not suitable for the embassy children to attend. The elite, including President Somoza, are educated in the United States. Their children have governesses and tutors through the elementary years and are usually sent to the United States to study by the time they reach high school. They often attend American Universities.

At first, a small group of us diplobrats are homeschooled by our mothers. I don't enjoy this arrangement, especially when my mother is the teacher. Eventually, Mother decides that there are other children in the American Embassy and various consulates who will be better served by attending classes in a more traditional setting. She organizes the mothers to start the American School. In 1944 this school was formally founded as the American Nicaraguan School, a coeducational, multicultural institution. The English speaking school with its American curriculum gained prestige and is still in existence today.

President Somoza of Nicaragua is a United States ally. He requests that the U.S. government send him a high ranking military officer to help start a military academy for his country. The U.S. sends him Colonel Roy Bartlett to head up the military academy. Military parades are held every week and I enjoy attending them. During these gatherings I learn all the military and patriotic songs.

There is also a military presence outside of Managua. They offer movies once a week. One evening I am watching the movie when I feel something soft and furry brush against my leg. I look down and find a little cat with a spotted coat resembling leopard print. He is so cute. I lift the kitty into my lap and began to pet him. He starts to purr. I decide to ask Mother to let me take him home. One of the soldiers comes up to me and suggests I should put the cat down. He explains the kitten is not a domestic cat. He is a "tiger cat," otherwise known as an oncilla, a small wildcat that lives in Central and South America. Oncillas usually make poor pets as they are difficult to domesticate and train. I reluctantly release him.

In Managua our family becomes good friends with the Finley family. The father, Dan Finley, is the assistant to the ambassador, his right hand man. The ambassador's residence sits on a hilltop surrounded by several acres of land. When the Finleys arrive, the ambassador insists they build a house with a swimming pool on his property. I spend time on the property watching the building of this home. Mr. and Mrs. Finley are nice and seem to enjoy having me around. They tell me they miss their son at Oxford University and jokingly offer to adopt me. My best friend Liana and I spend a lot of time at their home and in their swimming pool.

The second summer in Managua my family and Liana's family rent a summer home in San Juan del Sur, a coastal village on the Pacific Ocean. Today it is a well-known resort town, but in the early 1940s it was a simple fishing village with a few small farms. We enjoy playing on the beach and swimming in the ocean. We love to go horseback riding along the beach.

During the second week in San Juan del Sur my father becomes very ill. He calls his doctor in Managua who tells him penicillin is the most likely cure for his ailment. My father insists he will not be able to find penicillin in this little town. The doctor laughs, and then tells him to go to the nearest farm with chickens and offer to pay the farmer in exchange for penicillin. Daddy follows the doctor's orders and recovers quickly in spite of his qualms about taking chicken penicillin.

I also became friends with the daughter of a British family growing coffee on a plantation in the mountainous hills high above Managua. I visit her often on the beautiful plantation where the hillsides are lush and the mountain air is cool. I always have a good time.

On the last day of one of my visits my hosts decide it will be a fine adventure if we return to Managua on horseback. They have never ridden the trail before and insist it will be fun. The trip is a nightmare for all of us. There are long stretches of difficult terrain with narrow trails and steep cliffs along the way. An inexperienced rider, I don't know how to guide my horse down this dangerous terrain. The other riders can't help me because they are having problems too. Finally, I decide my horse doesn't want to fall down a hill or go over a cliff any more than I do; so I just pray and allow him to navigate the course.

We arrive safely at our destination, but only after an extremely distressing trip.

There were gold mines on the east coast of Nicaragua, most of which were run by or managed by American or British personnel. Bluefields, the largest city on the Nicaraguan Caribbean coast, was one of the centers of the mining industry. We make friends with a young couple from Britain. He is in a management position at one of the mining companies, spending the workweek at the company headquarters in Bluefields and returning to Managua on the weekends. His wife spends a lot of time with our family during the week. We exchange presents with them on Christmas Day. They give Mother a roll of pure gold. I receive a tiny pear shaped diamond. Mother decides she wants to use the gold to make a flower broach and place the diamond in the center. She draws a sketch so the jeweler can see the type of design she wants. Her rough draft turns out to be the finished article, size discrepancies and all! It is a unique and beautiful piece and we both enjoy wearing it.

1315 Elizabeth Blvd. – Childhood home of Chiquita Costen

Advertisement of 1315 Elizabeth Blvd.

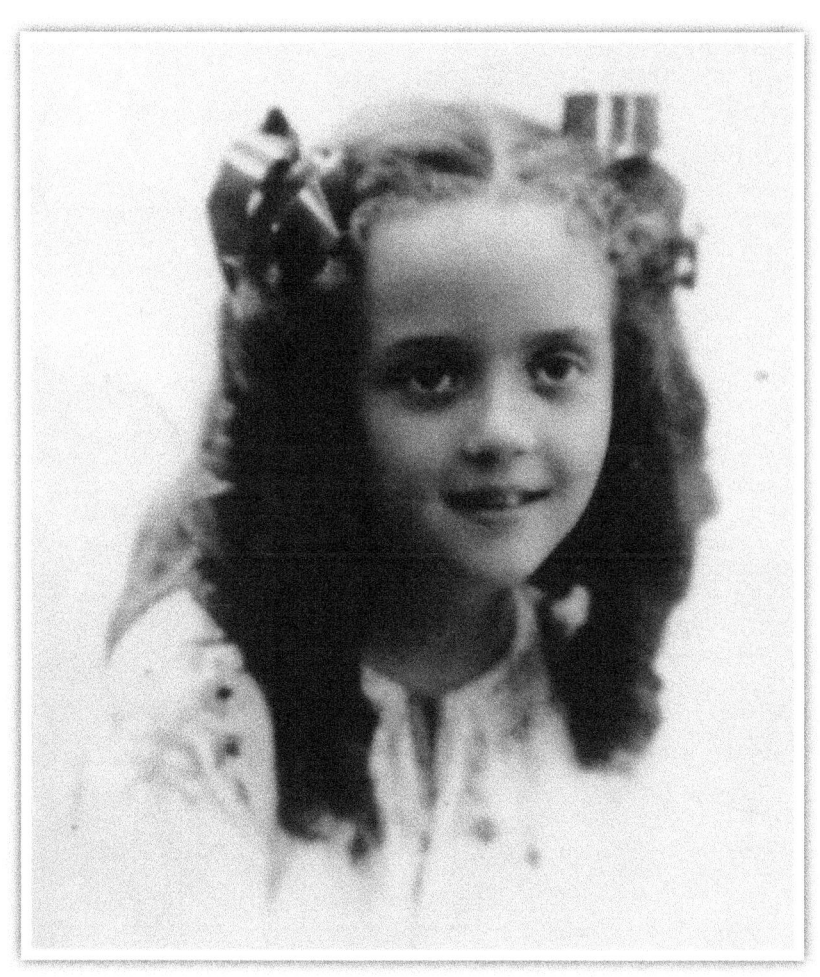

First Photo of Chiquita Costen

Chiquita with her father Jule

Chiquita with her mother Martha

Chiquita with her mother 'Mamita'

Brillantmont International School Since 1882 - Lausanne, Switzerland

Chiquita Costen Debutant Photo

Boeing 314 Clipper

Flying Clipper Map

Granddaughter with portrait of 'Mamita', Chiquita's mother Martha

Steeplechase Ball - Ridglea Country Club of Fort Worth - 1953

Return to Texas after Victory in Europe

Our family is still living in Nicaragua when Victory in Europe is declared. Church bells ring out and people are dancing and singing in the streets. After five long years the war in Europe is finally over. But, the war in the Pacific rages on.

Three weeks later, my father receives a letter from the State Department advising him of his new assignment: London, England. He is requested to leave Nicaragua with all haste in order to arrive at his new post immediately.

Mother is left in Nicaragua to make final arrangements and pack. She decides to send me ahead to my aunt and uncle's home in Corpus Christi, Texas.

In those days children traveling unaccompanied under the age of twelve were placed in the charge of flight attendants (airline stewardesses as they were called back then). I am just two weeks away from my twelfth birthday. The direct flight is to land in Brownsville, Texas where my aunt and uncle will be waiting for me.

On the way from Nicaragua to Texas, the plane develops some mechanical problems and is forced to land in Mexico City. A six hour delay is announced. I am tall for my age and look older so I am guided to a waiting bus with the other passengers. By the time the stewardesses look for me, I have been dropped-off at a busy square in the heart of downtown Mexico City and told to be back at 6:00 o'clock to return to the airport. I have a little money so I decide to get something to eat and sit on a bench to people watch until the bus comes back.

In the meantime, my aunt and uncle are waiting for me at the airport in Brownsville. They are concerned when the plane doesn't arrive on time and panic as the hours pass. No one has any information to give them regarding the flight delay. When the plane finally arrives, they are overjoyed to see me.

We drive to my aunt and uncle's home in Corpus Christi where I stay until my mother arrives a few weeks later. They have a son, my younger cousin Ligon, who has his own group of rowdy playmates in the neighborhood and shows little interest in me.

Corpus Christi is hot in the summer. My aunt and uncle arrange a comfortable place on the couch for me to sleep and place a big electric fan at the foot to blow cool air on me. My aunt also gives me some books to read. The stack includes several Bobbsey Twin books and a whole set of Nancy Drew mysteries. Outside of school assignments, I have never done much reading for entertainment. But Corpus is too hot and humid to do anything else. So I read a lot. I fall in love with Nancy Drew. I want to be Nancy Drew! That summer I develop my lifelong love of reading, especially mysteries.

My aunt and uncle remember my twelfth birthday on July 13, 1945 and we celebrate with a cake and candles. They give me a present, the latest Nancy Drew book. We go to the beach and I swim a couple of times. However, after being stung by an ocean creature known as a "jelly fish," I gladly return to the couch and read "just for fun."

Mother finally arrives in Texas and we return to Fort Worth. We stay for about month before receiving notification that we will be embarking from New York City on a transatlantic liner to Southampton, England to reunite with my father.

Arrival in England on Victory over Japan Day

Mother and I arrive at the piers in New York Harbor among a busy bustling throng that August afternoon in 1945, three months after Victory in Europe is declared by the United States and her allies. Anyone who could finagle a priority passage to Europe was trying to board the ocean liner setting sail for England that evening. The excited passengers, mingled with the crowds who had come to wave goodbye to their relatives and friends, almost makes getting on board a hazard.

As we make our way through the throngs of people, I think of the trip we previously made, from Lisbon to the United States, on the last clipper ship from Europe. Now we are returning to reunite with my father, a successful career diplomat assigned to London. Although I am twelve years old, Mother holds tightly to my hand, frantically looking for some people from the Red Cross she is scheduled to meet.

A month earlier, Mother receives a phone call from a Red Cross representative requesting she accompany three refugee children to England where they will be met by their parents. Anne, thirteen, her sister Frances, six, and her brother James, five, need to be chaperoned on the long ocean voyage. Senator Taft of Ohio and his wife are relatives of the children's mother and they were sent to live with the Taft family at the beginning of the bombings in England. The younger children were only two and three at the time. Only Anne has memories of her parents and her life in England. Now they will return, traveling with total strangers.

My mother's first reaction is utter dismay. The prospect of taking on the responsibility for a five year old boy on this high seas adventure seems daunting to her. She doesn't know anything about boys! The social worker assures her that Anne will be a big help as she has taken care of them all through the war. My mother, with great trepidation, agrees to chaperone the children.

We are looking at the crowd trying to find a couple with three children. I am eager to meet Anne as she is my age. Being an only child, I also have no idea of what to do with the younger ones! Somehow, the two families finally find each other among the noisy confusion and mass of humanity. Introductions are made, information is exchanged, and we are all hustled on board.

Anne and I are the lucky ones because we get to share a room. Our "luxury" liner is in the process of being reconverted from a troop ship and is anything but luxurious at this time. The crossing takes several days and goes very well. Anne and I become friends and the little ones are well-behaved. Once she gets used to having a little boy to contend with, my mother quite enjoys the little family. Even though the ship is a bare bones vessel, it does have one great amenity; a playroom where the little ones are taken care of all day long by registered nurses.

Anne and I are free to roam and we do. We meet another girl our age, Jeannie, who is returning to London with her family. We become a threesome and the cruise ship is our playground. We discover choppy seas are not to our liking and being out on deck in the fresh air is the best solution to queasiness. I don't think that prevents us from enjoying the wonderful buffets.

Finally the trip is winding down. We are all on deck, excitedly watching for land when the big announcement comes. THE WAR WITH JAPAN IS OVER! Japan has surrendered! Good news travels fast and a big cheer arises from the shore when we finally sight Southampton.

We dock amidst buntings and banners everywhere and are greeted as the great liberators! The bands play our American military songs and some of the old favorite, one of which is *Deep in the Heart of Texas*. Everyone taps and claps to this tune.

Anne's parents from Bristol are on hand for a joyful reunion with their children. They are incredibly grateful to my mother. Anne, Jeannie and I exchange hugs and promises of seeing each other soon.

A member of the U.S. Consulate in Southampton meets Mother and me and drives us to the train that will take us to London where my father will meet us. He has been living in a hotel for two months trying to find housing for the three of us. Everything is based on rank and priority. Even if you have a hotel room you can be bumped at any given moment by anyone who outranks you. London is teeming with military of all nations, but mostly Americans. Only essential personnel are allowed into the city. When I am older I learn that later, when my mother could handle it, she is told the only flat my father could find for us was in the Red Light District!

Everyone on the train is jubilant! It is V-J Day! Victory in Japan! The Japanese have finally surrendered. I don't understand the full significance of these events at that time, but am certainly aware of how much drinking and partying is going on all the way to London.

We arrive at London at dusk and are met by my father, who is stationed at the United States Embassy on Grosvenor Square. This is a four year assignment. With great delight he greets us. He winks at my mother as he tells me the British have put on a special welcome for us. As we approach the inner city we see fireworks and, true enough, it is the most lavish display I have ever seen. Having become use to the darkness of the war years, I have never seen such a show of brilliance. Glorious!

Eventually we near the flat my father has obtained for us only to have to make our way through throngs of jubilant people singing and drinking in the streets in celebration of the end of the war. Exhausted, we climb the stairs to the small flat and I plop into bed. I fall asleep quickly, but awakened by screeching at 3:00 a.m. I look out the window and see a woman standing underneath the lamppost loudly singing her version of *Lili Marlene.* I know and like the song, but this is too much! I jump back into bed and pull the pillow over my head.

The next morning at breakfast I am all excited because we are going to visit the Embassy where my father works. As we travel through London in the daylight we can see that much of the city is a bombed out disaster. I am shocked to see so much devastation. We arrive at Grosvenor Square, which was once a lovely park. It is now completely surrounded by coiled barbed wire. Gigantic anti-aircraft guns are emplaced all around as well as hastily built underground shelters guarded by soldiers in U.S. uniforms. I don't remember any buildings on the square that were destroyed, but there is evidence of their having been strafed by the German Luftwaffe.

I like being with Americans in the Embassy and will become very fond of the place during the next few years. It has dining facilities and a Post Exchange where we can buy all the things we could not otherwise purchase due to the severe rationing after the war.

To me, the highlight of my trip to England still remains that first night in London. I never forget the joy, excitement and fireworks of arriving in London in time to celebrate V-J Day! History was made that day and I felt a part of it!

First Months in London

During our first week in London, our large trunk arrives. Everything is damp, so Mother places it in front of the fireplace, pulls all the drawers out as far as possible, and leaves it overnight to dry out. Around midnight, it catches fire and what a ruckus ensues – firemen, buckets, and sirens! Finally the fire is out, but the stench is awful. My father calls in some favors and arranges for us to stay in a hotel for three days.

One person my mother never forgets is the char woman who cleans the flat. (In England the term *char woman*, derived from *chore woman*, refers to a house cleaner.) The char is a Cockney and speaks the Cockney dialect mainly spoken by Londoners of the working-class. The dialect has its own unique set of slang and expressions. Mother can hardly understand her. On her first day, Mother stresses that the woman should scrub the bathtub thoroughly because it is filthy. After the char leaves our flat that day, Mother checks the tub and finds it was still dirty. The next morning, she is ready to confront the char woman only to be answered in a loud Cockney voice saying it is too bad she doesn't like it but, "I never cleans beneath me own dirt!" Like it or not, that was that! So Mother scours it herself.

I go to the local elementary school there in the district. I walk up the narrow mews (streets where former stables have been converted into houses or flats) with a boy and girl who also go my way. Yes, they are both children of prostitutes, much to my mother's chagrin. I don't care. They are my friends!

I no longer remember what I did wrong in school, but my friend Robby takes the blame for whatever it was and receives a harsh caning for me. Caning, as administered at this school, is being repeatedly beaten on the open palm of your hand with a ruler. Robby never utters a word, but tears run down his face. I feel guilty and miserable. The children have decided to protect me from the harsh school master's ruler because I am new. It is years before I tell my parents about the incident, but you can believe I toe the line after that!

We stay in the district for eight months before finding a lovely home in Hatch End, a bedroom community in Pinner Parish, Middlesex just forty-five minutes out from London by train.

The Loveliness of Paris

Restrictions regarding travel between European countries gradually loosen after the war and my parents are eager to visit Paris. In January 1946 we fly from London to Paris. A driver is hired to take us into the city. The early evening is crisp and clear and my nose is pressed against the car window. We pass over the beautiful bridges that span the sinuous River Seine as it meanders through the heart of the city. I stare fascinated at the sights we pass in this fabled City of Light (La Ville Lumière). It is aglow with its glorious radiance. We come to the Place de la Concorde with the brightly spotlighted Obelisk in the center. Looking down the Champs de Elysee I can see the Arc de Triomphe, bathed in light and glowing like a star.

Just past the Place de la Concorde, we arrive at our hotel on the beautiful Rue de Rivoli in central Paris. Named for a Napoleon victory against the Austrian army, the area is known for its grand scale of architecture, commercial businesses, and many covered arcades. The Tuileries Gardens and the north wing of the Louvre are also on this street.

The next morning our sightseeing is a walking tour of the city. Like Londoners, Parisians are also living under harsh post-war restrictions and hardships. Money is scarce, factories on the outskirts of the city are bombed, industry is ruined, housing is in short supply, and severe rationing of food is in place. Unlike London, which is still in ruins as a result of the German bombing campaign during the war, the heart of Paris is intact.

I discover the Church of La Madeleine with its classical proportions, the Opera, the Eiffel Tower, and the view of the city from the Church of the Sacre Coeur. In the following days, I discover so much more of Paris. I fall in love, head over heels in love, with Paris.

The very mention of Paris evokes a visceral response. I have never lived there, but whenever I see her I feel as if I'm home again. What draws a person to a particular place? What causes this pull that continues to this day? I don't know. Maybe it has to do with being a part of my youth -- the carefree time of my life. Or perhaps there exists in my subconscious a place too strong to be denied.

Returning to Paris many times in my youth, I explore the city anew. As my French improves, I discover the theater of Racine and Moliere, the songs of Edith Piaf, the little sparrow with the husky voice, Montmartre and the Moulin Rouge; the whole spectrum that makes up Paris, and I become an avowed Francophile.

Youth is an emotional state and memories entwine, becoming inseparable. Each visit adds a memory -- staying with my godfather, a general on Eisenhower's staff, in his home under the shadows of the Eiffel Tower, getting to know native Parisians, joining my parents to celebrate Christmas at the home of some friends, and best of all, celebrating my eighteenth birthday in Paris.

The first time I visit Paris alone, my parents arrange for me to pick up an eighteenth birthday present at the American Embassy. The present is a box containing some lovely jewelry, which I wear that evening when family friends treat me to dinner at La Tour d'Argent. There is no more spectacular view of the back of the beautiful cathedral of Notre Dame de Paris, bathed in lights, than from the famous restaurant La Tour d'Argent. It is a perfect day that remains in my memory forever.

My last visit in my youth comes upon graduation from Mount Vernon Junior College. I fly from Washington D.C. to Paris where my parents join me and four of my friends to chauffeur us on an automobile tour of France and Spain.

Happy Days in England

In the fall I enroll in secondary school just before the beginning of the semester. It is a Catholic girls' school in Hatch End: The Immaculate Conception of Our Lady of Lourdes.

The required uniform is a pale blue color in the summertime and a darker blue in the winter, but mine is late in arriving. The first day of school I show up in a red plaid skirt with a red blouse. I stick out like a sore thumb, a humiliating experience for any thirteen-year-old girl. Fortunately the other girls are friendly and helpful and immediately make me feel welcome.

I learn to play lawn tennis, which is similar but also quite different from regular tennis. The Shakespearian classes are my favorites and the school has a school presentation of one of Shakespeare's plays every year. In the three years I am there, I am always cast as the male lead as I am the tallest girl in the class. Extensive memorization and practice is required for these productions. We also act out Biblical themes and stories. I love my Thespian years. The school day is long, although I don't recall a great deal of homework.

Classes at the convent start at 7:30 in the morning and I get home around 5:00 o'clock in the afternoon. I ride my bicycle to school. In the winter I go to school in the dark and return home in the dark. Car ownership after the war is extremely limited and most people rely on public transportation. Businessmen usually take the train into London. Only the very wealthy have limousines and chauffeurs.

So it is not unusual for me to ride my bicycle to school, even at dawn and dusk. Eventually, my parents acquire a Volkswagen. My mother is considered very much an independent American woman because she can drive a car!

My father loves being stationed in London. His boss is an old friend, whom he met when he was stationed in Argentina. He is a widower with two daughters; the younger daughter is my age. His older daughter helps with the entertainment and parties held in their home, but he is concerned that she is missing out on her own social activities. He offers my mother his entertainment allowance if she will take care of the dinner parties and she gladly accepts. This is compatible with her interests and qualifications; she loves to give dinner parties and everyone loves coming to her dinner parties where meat is always served. Great Britain has very strict rationing after the war. American diplomats can purchase meat and other commodities at the Post Exchange that are unavailable to the Brits.

My friend Jeannie, whom I met on the transatlantic voyage to Southampton, lives in London and I often take the train to visit her on weekends. Sometimes I spend the night and sometimes we just go to a movie and I return home in the afternoon. The train ride takes about 45 minutes. When I get back to my station, I have about a mile to walk to my home.

Our family has the opportunity to travel during the years we live in England. One winter our family takes a skiing trip to Megève, France near Mont Blanc in the French Alps. My parents invite Jeannie to go with us. We both become pretty good at the sport and have a wonderful time in the quaint and lovely town.

Anne's family lives in the town of Bristol in South West England. The first time I go to visit Anne I am introduced to a proper High Tea. While technically, afternoon tea may be taken at any time and is often less formal. The time for *High Tea* is four o'clock in the afternoon with rules and rituals that must be followed precisely. Anne's mother also teaches us how to play Mah Jongg. She learned the game while growing up in China, the daughter of missionaries. Anne, in turn, visits my home. I invite Anne to go on a two week family holiday to Italy. We spend a lot of time in the Italian countryside and end our trip in the fantastic city of Rome.

Mother loves Paris and loves to take trips for shopping or short vacations. I fall in love with Paris and it remains my favorite city in the world forevermore. We take in the sights of the city and enjoy watching the people while sitting in the bistros throughout the city. Mother also does some shopping while we are there. She loves the couture shops. She also loves hats and Paris is an amazing place to go if you love hats.

As I recall, Mother drives to Dover where we take the ferry to Dunkirk, then proceed to Paris via train. I remember coming home in our small Volkswagen with boxes underneath my feet, and a broom lying across my lap. Several plants that my mother wants for our home are scattered around in various spaces throughout the car.

By the time I turn fourteen, my parents and other members of the diplomatic corps decide that something needs to be done for the young people in our embassy and they start a teenage club in a section of Winfield House in Regent's Park, central London. This mansion, now the residence of the United States Ambassador to the United Kingdom, was built in the 1930's for heiress Barbara Woolworth Hutton. Commandeered and used by an RAF barrage balloon unit during the war, the beautiful home suffered significant damage. After the war the heiress donates it to the United States with the agreement that it will be restored and become the American Ambassador's residence in London.

The teenage club turns out to be a huge success. As I grow older, I attend some parties there, which Princess Margaret Rose, younger daughter of King George VI of England, also attends as she is dating a young American man.

I am invited to go to a feast for the Lord Mayor of London. A young man who is our neighbor is also invited and asks me to go with him.

So, I have my first so-called "date" at the age of fifteen. He sends me a corsage of tiny yellow orchids. Once we arrive the reception hall is crowded and we stand around talking to friends. My date speaks up to say, "I wonder where the old boy is?" The man in front of us turns around and smiles at us. Yes, the man in front of us is the Lord Mayor of London, a gracious, friendly man with a sense of humor who engages us in conversation while we wait.

All in all, England is quite an adventure for me and I love it there. Our whole family loves being stationed in Great Britain. We are disappointed when my father is assigned to be the Commercial Attaché in Budapest, Hungary.

Just before I leave London to travel to Budapest, a friend who attends the prestigious Eaton College invites me to celebrate the 14th of July with him at a formal event at his school. Yes, the 14th of July, also known as Bastille Day, is celebrated in the UK as well as in France. After dinner and prior to the evening fireworks, we have food and cold beverages at an outdoor event. It is amusing to see all the young men in tails and girls in formals having outside picnics.

The fireworks are the first Eton has displayed since the end of the war and they are spectacular! The most memorable fireworks display of the evening is as a dazzling portrait of the king and queen. It looks fabulous in brilliant bursts of light against the dark sky and a big cheer goes up from the crowd.

On The Way to Budapest

Daddy leaves for Budapest around the first part of May. Mother and I remain in England so I can complete the school semester. I am sorry to have to leave before I finish high school. My parents decide it is too far from Hungary to leave me as a boarding student in England.

A posting behind the Iron Curtain is considered a hardship post. Some wives do not accompany their husbands when they are assigned to these posts and few children are included in the Diplomatic Corps. The schools in Hungary are under communist control.

When the school year is over in England, Mother and I travel to Hungary by train, ferry boat, and automobile. I don't remember all the travel details, but do remember Mother acquires a car in Dieppe, France.

We visit some boarding schools in France and Switzerland on our way. In Switzerland we visit Brillantmont International School in Lausanne, one of the oldest boarding schools in Switzerland. Established in 1882 the secondary school follows the French curriculum. It is located in the center of Lausanne and the campus overlooks Lac Léman with the French Alps beyond. Arrangements are made for me to enter Brillantmont in the fall and we continue our journey to Budapest.

As we approach Vienna, Mother tells me that we are entering the Russian sector. At fifteen, I am initially oblivious to any problems that might present.

After we enter the zone occupied by Soviet Union troops, we are stopped at several different checkpoint stations by young Russian teenage soldiers carrying rifles. The sight of the armed soldiers and their repeated demands in Russian for our travel documents is intimidating, but there are no real concerns or unpleasantness. After getting past these checkpoints, we continue our drive to Budapest.

Driving through the countryside near the Hungarian border, we are surprised to be stopped at another checkpoint monitored by another young Soviet soldier who only speaks Russian. He motions for us to get out of the car. Mother tells me to stay in the car and she steps out to show him our papers. She produces our diplomatic passports and waves her hands as she tries to explain what she is holding. The young man glances at the documents, but keeps looking over at me. At this point another teen-age soldier with a machine gun joins them. Some kind of conversation appears to take place between the three of them. Finally, the first soldier returns our passports to my mother and we continue on our way to Budapest.

Budapest: City of Romance, Mystery and Intrigue

In mid-June Mother and I arrive in the legendary city of Budapest on the Danube, fabled throughout the centuries for its beauty. My arrival in London in 1945 has exposed me to the decimations of warfare, and bombings and it is obvious Budapest also suffered great damage during the war. Although the vestiges of beauty still remain and reconstruction is in progress, every area of this lovely city shows signs of ravage and neglect.

From the day we arrive, the Hungarians prove to be a warm, friendly, welcoming people who love good food, good music, and longtime traditions. They are also a people who love their country. It is sad their beloved country is now behind the Iron Curtain, the citizens living under the cruel and oppressive shadow of communism.

The Hungarian capital is primarily the unification of two cities, Buda and Pest. The Danube River flows between their banks. Budapest was created in 1872 when the ancient cities of Pest, Buda, and Óbuda were united into a single municipal borough. Buda is built on a hill on the Western bank of the Danube and is the historical part of the city. Pest, on the Eastern bank of the river, is on a flatter plain and has more businesses, shopping and boulevards. You can cross between the two different parts of the city on magnificent bridges. There is a small island in the middle of the Danube River between the shores of Buda and

Pest. The island, which is quite lush, is called Margaret's Island and is connected to both sides of Budapest by a lovely old arched bridge.

Our family will be living in a home the American Embassy is providing on the Buda side of the Danube. However, until our furniture arrives we will be temporarily staying in a graceful old hotel on Margaret's Island surrounded by formal gardens. It is the most luxurious hotel that Budapest can offer and the only one where foreigners are allowed to stay.

On our first evening in Budapest, we have dinner near our hotel on Margaret's Island. It is a beautiful evening and we are seated outside by a uniformed waiter. Where we are seated overlooks a beautiful garden. Dinner, in the summertime, is served late and the dusk fades into night as lanterns glow. They surround us with soft light, creating a mellow mood. The Gypsy violins start to play and soon everyone is dancing and clapping to the rhythm of the lively strains. The musicians alternate from joyous dance music to soulful cries, artfully drawn from the violins. It is a beautiful, welcoming, romantic evening that seems to be made perfect for one American teen-age girl.

After dinner our family takes a stroll through the gardens before retiring to our rooms. Mother and I listen to my father as he explains to us the dangers of living in this communist controlled country. Nothing is to be discussed within the confines of the walls.

He cautions: "The rooms are bugged. I even know where they can be found! If anything important needs to be said it must be whispered in the bathroom with the shower running at full blast. Nothing of note must even be discussed inside the hotel or in any other building. Out of doors, and out of earshot provides the greatest degree of safety."

The warnings of my father bring a reality that overshadows the happiness of the lovely evening.

During the time we live on Margaret's Island waiting for our furniture and household goods to arrive from London, Mother and I spend our days exploring Budapest, getting acquainted with embassy personnel, and meeting the other diplomatic corps families.

The Swiss Ambassador has a thirteen-year-old daughter, as well as an older son on vacation from the University of Zurich spending the summer in Budapest. The British Ambassador, a single parent, has his twelve-year-old son for the summer, and one of his attaches has three young daughters. There are no schools in Budapest that are appropriate for western diplobrats to attend. Classes are all taught in either Hungarian or Russian and they are all public schools under Communist direction.

We also meet our future across-the-street neighbor Don, a United States Air Force pilot. He is a young, handsome, single attaché who flies the Embassy plane. His house is a large three-story building hanging on the downside of a hill on the Buda side.

Finally our furniture arrives and we move into a lovely home high in the hills of Buda. The home is situated on several acres of land and has wonderful views. Due to the topography of the Buda hills, the house is built into the side of the hill with the single car garage being part of the basement. The home also comes with a swimming pool – more like a large pond by today's standards.

One feature of our home is quite unique, especially considering the availability of land around the home. In order to get to the garage, you have to drive up a long hilly driveway. As you approach the garage there is a stone retaining wall on the left. You have to make a sharp right turn to enter the garage. Once inside you find yourself on an enormous turntable which has to be hand cranked to rotate the car. Backing out is impossible!

The hills surrounding our home in Buda are lush and green and the soil is well-drained. The sloping fields are covered in wildflowers, and flowers are well-attended within the yards.

On our property there is a large field of poppies growing outside of the servants' quarters. By the beginning of July a sea of white, red and purple blossoms create a beautiful landscape.

One morning we are surprised to find we are being raided by the Hungarian police who are in the poppy fields shouting, in Hungarian of course, to each other and to the servants. My mother goes out to meet the authorities who begin to scythe the poppies down and cart off the remains. She doesn't understand why there is a problem; she thinks the blossoms are lovely.

It turns out the servants are raising the poppies for the opium they produce. The servants are not arrested, but let off with a stern warning. It is their very good fortune to be working for Embassy personnel with diplomatic immunity!

Spies are everywhere in Budapest. We share a civilian maid with our across-the-street neighbor Don. She is a known spy for the communist government. She doesn't spy on us out of any malice or political conviction. She doesn't have a choice.

Any civilian who works for a member of the diplomatic corps, or in any capacity that might allow him or her to overhear conversations or discover items of interest is expected to "spy" on their employers. Severe punishments are meted out to those who refuse or fail in this assignment.

In the beginning, my mother and Don find it amusing to discuss fabricating some information to "leak" in front of the maid. However, early on we discover that she is being beaten when she has nothing consequential to report. Any harmless amusement they might have imagined through this game quickly turns to real concern and genuine sympathy for this decent civilian trying her best to work and survive under a cruel post-war regime.

I will never forget the first time she shows up with a black eye and bruises over her body and tells us "it is nothing." She is very taciturn and refuses to discuss it even though she cannot hide the black and blue marks on her neck and legs. Her long-sleeved uniform hides the ones on her arms and neck.

This lady is definitely of higher social strata and is another victim of the circumstances in which she now finds herself. She seems afraid of the other servants and of us. Her previous pleasantness and passable English become nonexistent. The communists are undoubtedly threatening her with dire consequences, or harm to either her parents or to her children, if she does not cooperate.

To our distress we learn this goes on all the time in Budapest. There is nothing we can do to help her. The basic objective of the communist government is to facilitate the creation of a communist dictatorship. Real or perceived enemies of the regime must be identified and dealt with harshly. This type of hardship assignment causes immense strain on both families and singles in the diplomatic corps. A heavy toll is exacted when you have to watch your every word, fear for your safety, and know you cannot reach out to help others in need.

In England I had the routine of school and enjoyed many friendships and social activities. I also enjoyed a great deal of independence and freedom. My parents allowed me to travel alone by train to London and stay over with friends when I attended dances and other events. There is nothing for a young person of my age to do alone in Budapest. I have no friends my own age. Mother and I explore the city and historical sites. I accompany my parents to all of the cocktail parties, nightclubs and dinners with the adults. I don't drink, but I love to dance. My father and family friends, gallantly indulging my eagerness to be on the dance floor, invite me to foxtrot or waltz. My favorites are the high energy songs.

The Embassy is guarded by the Marines. I will turn sixteen in July and some of the young guards are only a few years older. When I am at the Embassy I enjoy visiting with them and they seem to enjoy laughing and joking with a young American girl.

Bob, a young handsome Marine guard, invites me out and I am eager to accept. The Americans associated with the Diplomatic Corps form a little community in Budapest and are acquainted with one another. My parents proceed to question the young Marine guard as to where he intends to take me. He says he would like to take me out to a nightclub for dinner and dancing.

My mother hesitates to allow her not quite sixteen-year-old daughter to go out to a nightclub. Dinner is served late in Budapest and dancing will go on into the early morning hours. I, of course, point out the fact I have been going out to nightclubs with them for the past several weeks.

My mother turns to my father, "Jule, do you agree that it is okay for them to go to a nightclub?"

My father speaks up, "It will have to be okay, because there isn't any other place in Budapest that would be safe to take her!"

The night of the anticipated event arrives and my mother is still worrying. She admonishes the young Marine not to keep me out too late.

He replies, "Don't worry Mrs. Smith, I'll get her home. I have to report for duty at zero 800 hours."

Off we go. I have a perfectly wonderful evening and feel very grown up and sophisticated. My date is handsome, attentive and a good dancer. We have a lot of fun and he returns me home by the appointed time of 1:00 am.

Later, Mother comes into my bedroom to tell me goodnight. "Did you have a good time tonight," she asks.

"Yes, I had a wonderful time," I reply. "I'm not a bit tired. Mamita, I could have gone on dancing forever!"

The following morning Mother leaves for Pest to run some errands and stops by to see my father. Upon her arrival outside the Embassy, she sees Bob who is relieved of guard duty to go to lunch. He is limping slightly and has a sickly-looking complexion. Mother is concerned and stops as they pass on the plaza.

"Bob, are you feeling well?" She inquires.

"Oh, Mrs. Smith," replies Bob, "I'm just worn out from dancing. My feet are killing me. I've never seen a girl who enjoys dancing so much. We had a great evening, but every time a song ended and I thought we would sit down another song started and Chiquita wanted to keep dancing. She could have gone on dancing forever. I'm just too old and decrepit to date a fifteen-year-old."

Mother enjoys repeating that story for years to come!

In July my sixteenth birthday is celebrated. Some celebrations of special occasions are exceptional and that evening seems magical to me. Dinner is wonderful and the gypsy violins and subtle lighting set the mood for deep feelings of happiness.

I feel safe and secure and connected with the adults gathered around me at the table. At that moment in time, I contemplate the possibility that all my hopes and dreams for the future will surely come true. Anything seems possible.

Don gives me a large bottle of Chanel #5 perfume, which to me is the epitome of sophistication and elegance. My father's secretary's gift is three small floral pieces of Herend china, which I cherish to this day. Mother's gift to me is a silver and crystal dresser set, which I in turn am privileged to pass on to my daughter on her sixteenth birthday. Daddy's gift is a lovely ring of two entwined diamonds, which he picked out for me. The two diamonds from this special gift became my two daughters-in-law's engagement rings.

Don is dating a Hungarian beauty named Itsa. She is petite, dark, and looks like a movie star. Don is tall, dark and handsome and they make a stunning couple, particularly on the dance floor. They are wonderful dancers. Even with her stiletto heels, petite Itsa barely reaches to Don's shoulders. He knows, too, that she is a spy; she has to be a spy. He still falls deeply in love with her and his love is returned.

As I go to all of the cocktail parties and dinners with the adults, I enjoy spending more and more time with Don and Itsa. Our entire family falls in love with the lovely Itsa and wishes the best for her and Don.

Don and Itsa confide in my parents. They are in love and want to spend the rest of their lives together. They ask my parents to consider the options with them. They discuss Itsa leaving the country, but come to the understanding that her communist bosses would never allow her to leave Hungary. If she manages to get out on her own, her family remaining in Budapest might suffer severe retributions by the communist government.

The best course for them is to get married so Don can obtain an

American passport for her as his wife. They acknowledge that even this plan may fail. Don decides when he makes one of his trips to Vienna he will find out what can be done at the American end to help them.

Just before I leave for school in August, Don returns from Vienna. He comes over to our home to show us a set of rings he bought on his trip. The news in Vienna is encouraging. He is going to ask Itsa to marry him. He radiates happiness as he contemplates their future together. I feel so happy for Don and Itsa and so honored to be shown the rings Don plans to give her.

That very day Itsa disappears. It seems she disappears off of the face of the earth. Don, and Itsa's family, desperately try to find her. He explores every avenue and even goes to Communist Headquarters in his quest. In this record-crazy communist police state, where everything is known about everybody, no one claims to have ever even heard of her.

Itsa is never again seen or heard from, and Don and her family are devastated. We are all devastated by this tragedy.

Itsa's disappearance has a tremendous impact on my life and in the weeks after her disappearance I think of her constantly. I am no longer the carefree child feeling so safe and sheltered by loving parents. Living in a communist controlled country becomes both oppressive and scary to me.

Tension cannot be maintained indefinitely and sometimes I momentarily forget, relax, and enjoy the novelty of living in the beautiful city of Budapest. And then something happens, a chance word or warning that reminds me of the dangers of this assignment. I am ready to leave Budapest and go off to school. I am ready for my parents to leave this assignment.

Never again will I read a mystery story or spy thriller without remembering the uncertainty, intrigue, and heart breaking tragedy our family experienced in a communist controlled country behind the iron curtain. Real life is so often stranger than fiction!

School in Switzerland

I leave Budapest in mid-August to attend Brillantmont International School in Lausanne, Switzerland. I plan to return to Budapest during the winter break to spend the Christmas holidays with my parents. Despite the existing tensions, it has been a remarkable summer. I still cling to the hope Itsa will return to Don and her family and there will be a happy ending to the story. The happy ending never comes. Don eventually marries and has three lovely daughters. But he never sells the rings that he bought for Itsa.

Don flies Mother and me to Paris on the Embassy plane and the flight is spectacular. He invites me to sit in the co-pilot's seat as we fly low over the countryside and on to Paris, my favorite city in the entire world. The summer day is clear and crisp and the aerial views are incredible. As we approach Paris the beautiful capital city appears to actually sparkle in its loveliness. The details of the flight remain in my memory forever.

I love being in Paris again where Mother and I spend a couple of days strolling through the city, taking in some Parisian sights, and dining at classic bistros. Mother rents a car for the trip to Lausanne. I think she enjoys this brief escape from the underlying stresses of my father's diplomatic post in Budapest. She seems relieved that I will be living in the cloistered atmosphere of a small private Swiss school. Still, I sense she has some trepidation about leaving me at a new school among girls I have never met. She asks me to write her regularly and expresses her hope that I will be happy in Lausanne.

When we arrive at Brillantmont, we are graciously greeted by the faculty and I start meeting other arriving students. It is the first time since returning to Europe that I have been with so many American girls, although the school is composed of girls of many nationalities. As an only child spending the summer with my parents in Budapest, I miss the close camaraderie of friends my own age.

My room-mate is an Indian girl with the nickname *Coochi*. She is related to the Maharaja of Cooch Behar, hence her nickname. My suite-mates are American, Canadian, and Italian. Our rooms are small, but adequate and the views from our dorm room windows are spectacular. The school is located on a hill overlooking Lac Leman. Across the lake we could see the town of Evian, France and the Alps beyond it.

We live in a building called *Dix-Huit* (Eighteen). Our building is connected to the main building by a second story passageway. Our classes are held in the main building and beyond that building are two other buildings. One is mostly inhabited by British girls. The other building is reserved for girls who are already eighteen years of age or older as many girls attend Brillantmont's prestigious finishing school after completing high school. Princess Ragnhild of Norway lives in that building.

The classes at Brillantmont were all held in French and we were not supposed to speak any other language. English seemed to be the most popular second language and we girls managed to develop a dialect we called "Fringlish."

I write glowing letters home telling my parents how much I enjoy the school and my classmates and all of the activities, and how much fun I am having. Mother reads my glowing letters for six weeks and wonders if I am covering up my homesickness, loneliness, and misery. She concludes: "She doth protest too much!"

Mother travels to Lausanne to check on me and I am overjoyed to see her. I introduce my lovely Mamita with pride to my friends. Mothers are universally special; truth be told, we all miss our mothers. The girls make every attempt to welcome her, engage her in conversation, and include her in activities. Satisfied that I am well and happy, Mother returns to Budapest, possibly a little disappointed that I display not a smidgen of homesickness.

As the Holidays approach, I look forward to returning to Budapest to celebrate Christmas with my parents. Sadly, I never see Budapest again.

Persona Non Grata

Shortly before Christmas I receive a telegram; plans have changed. I will meet my parents in Paris and we will spend the holidays with family friends. Travel arrangements are explained, but no explanation is given for the change of plans.

I don't hear from my parents again until I arrive in Paris. During this time, I can only wait and worry for updates on their status. I learned from Itsa's disappearance how dangerous it can be to live in a communist controlled country.

What my parents couldn't tell me is that Jule is declared "persona non grata" by the Communist government in Hungary. He is accused of being a spy and given twenty-four hours to get out of the country.

In diplomacy a 'persona non grata' is a person not welcome in a foreign host country. The host country may declare *persona non grata* status for any member of the diplomatic corps at any time, for any reason, and without any explanation. This is a serious charge. The host country can take away diplomatic immunity to a *persona non grata*.

My parents make haste to leave the country. Don flies them to Vienna, Austria on the Embassy plane. The plan is for them to continue to Paris via train. When my parents arrive in Vienna in 1949, Austria remains under joint occupation of the Western Allies and the Soviet Union. The American Intelligence Branch in Vienna debriefs Jule. They determine that he is the bearer of information so sensitive that it will not be safe for him on the train as it travels through the communist controlled Russian sector. The Russians might suspect he is the bearer of secrets and *intellegencia* and seize him for interrogation.

Two days later my parents are flown to Paris in a military plane and invited to stay with dear family friends who have an apartment in the city. They pick me up at the train station when I arrive and spend the next couple of days explaining what they couldn't tell me before we were together in person.

I am relieved and overjoyed they are once again in non-occupied Europe.

Christmas in Paris and Summer in Stockholm

A few days later we celebrate Christmas with our friends. They have a twelve-year-old son and our host family is warm, welcoming, and pleasantly cheerful. The two families have a lot of fun together.

After a wonderful Christmas dinner, the presents are handed all around and we begin to open them. The first present I open is a middle-sized box that contains a lovely gray squirrel cape and I am delighted. We continue to open other presents and I am handed a large box. Lo and behold it contains a sheared beaver Eisenhower-style jacket, a very popular fashion item for that time. We are served hot chocolate as we continue unwrapping until the presents are almost gone. My father picks up a very large box and walks over to me.

"Chiquita, can you guess what is in this box?"

Well, I couldn't, so I just open it. And then I start squealing. It was the most beautiful black, full length baby lamb designer coat I had ever seen. After all these years, I still have it and it is still the loveliest design I have ever seen! I refer to that Christmas as "my very furry Christmas!"

A few days after Christmas I return to Lausanne to go to a skiing resort with several other girls from Brillantmont. We stay in a large wooden cabin, a chalet, in the mountains around the ski resort of Villars.

I love to ski and have a wonderful time on the trip. We do a lot of skiing and the weather is fair and sunny in spite of low temperatures. We get quite warm on the slopes and end up wrapping our jackets around our waists. We also manage to get sunburned.

In the evenings we are tired and ready to sit around the massive fireplace in our flannel nightwear while talking, reading, and enjoying hot chocolate. I also remember having my first pizza on this trip. One of the Italian girls offers to make it for all of us one evening and it becomes an instant favorite for the group.

My father's new assignment is Stockholm, Sweden. The city of Stockholm is a unique and beautiful capital. It is situated on fourteen islands and has many beautiful bridges and canals connecting the city.

When school is out I invite my best friend from school, Monique, to go to Sweden with me for two weeks. I have previously spent some time in Monique's home in the South of France.

Mother plans some sightseeing for us and we enjoy exploring the city and the many summer activities of this Nordic country.

My friends from the transatlantic voyage from New York to Southampton, Anne and Jeannie, also come to visit that summer. I remember returning the visits and going on some trips with them. I celebrate my seventeenth birthday in Stockholm on July 13, 1950. Anne and Jeannie are there for my birthday and two young men, one is English and other one is French, show up for the celebration.

One of the young men is a family friend who is staying with us for a couple of weeks. His parents own a publishing business in London and he is in Sweden to visit pulp plants. Summer is the best time to visit Sweden with its long days, beautiful fields of flowers, unique water ways, magical destinations, and outdoorsy culture.

I enjoy a relaxed and casual summer in Sweden and the weeks pass quickly.

Skiing Accident at Villars

I return to Lausanne in the fall for my last year of high school. My second year at Brillantmont I live in the main house. I take some extra courses to prepare for the French Civil Service Exams, and work hard to get through all of my classes.

One Saturday morning in January, I board a train at the railway station in Lausanne with a group of girls from Brillantmont. Loaded with ski equipment we travel to the neighboring town of Villars, a popular ski resort. We plan to spend the day on the slopes and return to Brillantmont in the evening. That afternoon, I am enjoying a run down one of the slopes when I fall. In those days we do not have release bindings and our skis are over six feet long. Most injuries occur when skiers try to get up from a fall because the skis are so unmanageable. When I try to get up my skis get tangled and I fall forward, injuring both my foot and knee. My friends catch up with me and summon the ski patrol. The patrol places me on a stretcher and delivers me to an ambulance near the ski lifts. My foot and knee are examined. They are bruised and swelling, but nothing is broken. While I am being bandaged, the medical staff gives me some instructions on caring for my injuries. The emphasis is "stay off that leg!"

I don't recall how I make it back to school, but I am promptly put to bed and remain there for several days. My meals are served in my room. My teachers come by after classes bringing hot chocolate along with up-dates on my assignments. In the evenings my room becomes a gathering place for my friends. During the long afternoons, I have the luxury of reading "for fun." In spite of this splendid time of rest and recuperation, I am glad to go back to my classes. Walking with a limp and wearing fuzzy house shoes, my days on the ski slopes are over for the semester.

Presentation at the Court of Saint James's

Mother tries to avoid the expense of sending telegrams so I am surprised to receive one at Brillantmont. The other girls are curious and gather around as I read it. The brief wording informs me I am to meet my mother in Paris, shop for a special dress, and then proceed to London to be presented to King George VI and the royal family.

I arrive at the train station in Paris and hire a taxi to take me to the hotel to meet my mother. It is springtime and the parks and gardens of the city are filled with flowers in all the colors of the rainbow. The city is indeed beautiful.

I meet my mother at her hotel and she shows me the "summons" I have received from the Lord Chamberlain.

The Lord Chamberlain is
commanded by Their Majesties to summon
Miss Martha Smith
to an Afternoon Presentation Party at Buckingham Palace
on Wednesday the 14th March from 3:30 to 5:30 o'clock p. m.

We have a quick lunch at a favorite bistro before starting our rounds of the couture houses. In the past I visited such places with mother in Paris, but never for me. This time it is for me!

We arrive at the first house and are graciously seated. And then starts the parade of dresses, the presentation dress being the most important. I really like the second one out, so I try it on. It is a beautiful steel blue silk taffeta and fits me perfectly. This is definitely the one. This is the dress! It is ankle length and full. The top is asymmetrical and one shoulder is bare-with a ruffle for a sleeve. This ruffle turns into a deep fold that goes straight across to the other shoulder. This shoulder has a wide ruffle overshadowing the shoulder almost like a small umbrella. It is perfect in my eyes.

Mother has different ideas about the presentation dress and reminds me we need to go to some of the other stores to see what they have to offer. Besides, she thinks the dress needs to be more discrete and not so *cocktailish*. So off we go to look at more dresses. I try on several, but still prefer the first one. Mother finally calls it quits and we go back to the first shop and buy the dress I want. We also purchase two other dresses Mother considers "simple, elegant, and appropriate" for many occasions. One of the purchases, my first black dress, is a Jacque Fath "creation." Fath, a popular postwar haute couture designer, is known for dressing the "chic young Parisienne."

One more important item is necessary. A hat! Thank goodness Mother loves hats and knows several shops. By the time we make it to the third shop we are both exhausted. But, that's where we find it: a Juliette cap with tiny pink flowers and green leaves mounted on mesh that sits snuggly on the back of my head. On my dark brown hair it looks young and different.

The shoes are the problem. Due to the ski accident earlier in the year I am still wearing ballerina-like slippers to my classes. I worry about the deep curtsy I will make to King George and the royal family. I am scared my knee will give out and I will fall flat on my face! The beautiful high heels that will make the presentation ensemble perfect are out of the question.

A String of Pearls

The next day Mother and I are off to London to meet my father. Once at the hotel, we start looking through her shoes to find a pair I might wear to the presentation. We find some moderately low, sensible-looking blue suede wedge heels. I practice walking in them. It is a challenge.

The morning after we arrive we have a ten o'clock appointment at Clarence House to meet one of the ladies-in-waiting to Princess Elizabeth. Clarence House is where Prince Phillip and Princess Elizabeth live with their two children. The lady-in-waiting, who had made the arrangements for us to meet, is a cousin to a dear family friend of ours with whom we were stationed in Budapest. As we enter the house there is a glass wall in front of us that overlooks a small enclosed garden where a baby carriage sits on the lawn. The man escorting us says Princess Anne is getting her daily fresh air.

At that moment a small boy with a stick horse comes barreling down the staircase with a frantic Nanny in tow. She catches up with him and apologizes for the disruption. He is cute and so we all laugh. Of course it is a very young Prince Charles, currently King Charles III of England. Hearing the commotion, the lady we are here to see comes out and greets us.

We have a lovely early morning tea as she explains to us all what will be taking place at court the following morning. The lady herself is charming with a delightful sense of humor, so we have a most enjoyable morning.

On the morning of the presentation, I go to the Embassy and meet the American Ambassador. Then I am whisked off to Buckingham Palace in a limousine. I am ushered in by a side door and escorted into a large waiting room filled with other girls who are being presented that afternoon. I feel intimidated by my surroundings. I think all the girls are nervous. We can't see what is going on in the presentation hall and we have to wait a couple of hours before we are announced, one-by-one, to be presented.

Finally it is my turn. The door to the massive hall opens and I see a wide expanse of wood flooring crossing between where the spectators, including my parents, are sitting and the raised dais where the King and the royal family are seated. I realize *this is the moment*. I am going to fall flat on my face!

As I am announced, I walk straight toward the dais. Princess Margaret Rose appears bored. I stop before King George VI, and look directly at him. He seems to be straightening his collar. I extend my arms to my sides and lower my chin while remembering to maintain eye contact. Catching the sides of my dress and placing my right foot behind my left, I slowly bend my knees and lower myself, briefly hold the position, and then slowly straighten my knees as I return to a standing position with my back straight.

I cross the rest of the room trying to maintain a look of confidence and poise and manage to exit through the designated door. I find myself in a large hallway and breathe a sigh of relief. An attendant escorts me into a banquet room where waiters are serving champagne and hors d'oeuvres. I have been too nervous to eat before the presentation. I have some finger sandwiches and mingle a little with the other young girls and their families. My parents also attend this event.

Returning to my hotel, I prepare for the presentation ball that evening. Several more events are on the agenda for the week, but this is the only one I will attend as I must return to Brillantmont to resume my studies.

That evening I am escorted by a charming young family friend, Simon. Several years my senior, Simon has escorted other young ladies to presentation balls and appears to feel confident in this surrounding. He is an excellent dancer. Before the evening is over, I am having a wonderful time; worries about my wobbly knee and falling flat on my face are in the past!

The following morning I return to Lausanne and spend the next few weeks reviewing for the upcoming finals. At the end of the semester, I pass the French Civil Service Exam as well as all of the final proficiency exams. I leave Brillantmont with optimism as I look toward the future.

Postscript

After Brillantmont, I return to the United States and enroll in Mount Vernon Junior College in Washington D.C. Today this campus is known as the Mount Vernon Campus of George Washington University. I enjoy being back in the United States and living in the nation's capital. During this time my father retires and my parents buy a home in Mallorca, Spain, a large island in the western Mediterranean.

To celebrate my graduation from Mount Vernon, my parents arrange a driving trip through parts of Europe for me and four friends. Three of us, American girls, fly to Paris where my parents meet us with two young family friends, European girls, who accompany us on this grand touring excursion. We have a wonderful time. After a week in Paris, we tour the French countryside and then spend another week touring Spain. I spend the rest of the summer with my parents in Mallorca.

My parents plan to return to Texas. Mother decides she wants me to be presented as a debutante at the Assembly Presentation Ball in Fort Worth, and considers this an opportunity for me to meet other Fort Worth girls and their families.

In Fort Worth there are two social clubs that date back to the early 1900s. Each year both clubs present young women making their debuts into society. One is the women's club, Assembly. And the other is the men's' club, the Steeplechase. The debutantes are presented at annual presentations balls. A young woman making her debut is usually sponsored by a previous debutante of the social club, traditionally by her mother, grandmother, or aunt. I am sponsored by one of my paternal aunts. As it turns out, I am presented at both the Assembly Ball at Rivercrest Country Club and the Steeplechase Ball at Ridglea Country Club in 1953. There are several weeks of social events preceding the presentations.

A modified curtsy called "the Texas dip" is the mainstay of Texas debutantes. One legend surrounding this elaborate curtsy says it is the maneuver famed ballerina Anna Pavlova made as her depiction of a dying swan in a 1909 ballet. Another story claims it is a variation of the St. James Bow, first performed by young ladies to honor Queen Victoria. Regardless of origin, it is an intricate curtsy; a tricky maneuver requiring serious practice.

The night of the Assembly presentation ball arrives. When the announcer calls my name I walk onto stage. Beautiful music plays in the background and glaring lights almost blind me. I perform the challenging "Texas dip," and taking my escort's hand, manage to stand back up. We proceed down to the dance floor where we watch the remaining presentations. After the last girl is presented, the debutantes are presented as a group and led to the center of the dance floor by their escorts for the first dance. About halfway through the dance, my handsome daddy cuts in and leads me in a graceful waltz across the room. It is my favorite memory of the evening!

My parents move to Fort Worth where they resume old friendships and acquaintances and make many new friends. They celebrate more than fifty years of marriage.

I meet George Foster and we fall in love. George is an aeronautical engineer and a graduate of the University of Texas. He works at General Dynamics, Fort Worth's large historic "bomber plant" that began operations in 1942 as Consolidated Aircraft. Today it is known as Lockheed Martin.

George and I marry in 1955. We have a beautiful wedding at St. Andrew's Episcopal Church and make our home in Fort Worth. I become active in the Junior League of Fort Worth and The Junior Woman's Club of The Woman's Club of Fort Worth.

George and I are blessed with four children, three boys and a girl, George, Tom, Marian, and Ned. I am busy through the years taking care of my family. I am involved with the children's school activities, their participation in sports and other events, and encouraging their pursuits of their own special interests. There are many memorable occasions celebrated through the years. I carry a large calendar book everywhere to help me keep track of the comings and goings of my family. My parents adore the grandchildren and the sentiment is mutual.

After almost twenty-five years of marriage, George and I decide to go our separate ways. The divorce is amicable. Our children are reaching their young adult years; pursuing their educational aspirations, careers, engagements, and marriages. I soon find myself becoming an empty nester.

I remain active in The Woman's Club of Fort Worth, joining the Mah Jongg Department, the Language Department where classes in conversational French and Spanish are offered, the Beaux Arts Club, and the Art Department where I pursue my love for acrylic painting, while still remaining active in the Shakespeare Club and the Creative Writing Department. I join friends for luncheons in the Woman's Club Tea Room several times a week.

Active and busy, I am sure I will never again marry. Then, one fine day, I meet Constantin Costen. Connie, as he is called, is a retired Air Force Lieutenant Colonel. He served in the military for 22 years. An engineer by profession, Connie also works at General Dynamics.

Connie and I find we have interests in common and enjoy spending time together. We fall in love. He asks me to marry him; I say, "Yes."

Connie and I both love to travel. He knows I love Paris, although I have not returned to that beautiful city since my graduation from Mount Vernon. He arranges a trip to Europe for our Honeymoon with Paris as our prime destination.

For more than thirty years the only Paris I knew lived in my memories and, perhaps, in my imagination. It is with joy I look forward to returning after so long an absence. I also feel some trepidation. So much has changed in thirty years, including me. I wonder what I will discover. Will the reality of modern day Paris attract me? Will the city be degraded with tall metal and glass skyscrapers, and the golden arches of McDonalds? What will I find?

Boarding the train at Calais, my excitement mounts as Connie and I head toward Paris. We arrive at the Gare St. Lazare at dusk in a downpour. No longer fluent in French, I nevertheless manage to direct a taxi driver to out small hotel close to the Eiffel Tower. We drive through the central part of the city to our destination. At once I feel as if I've come home again at long last. Even in the rain Paris is beautiful.

To my immense pleasure and relief I find the city of my memory unchanged. Yes, there are some modern buildings located some distance away from the center of Paris, but the heart of the city is intact. McDonald's does exist on the Champs de Elysee, but discreetly among the myriad of shops and cafes that line that most famous boulevard. The chic Parisians can still be spotted among the jean-clad youth, and the language still sounds beautiful to my ears.

The changes are subtle. I do miss the kepi policeman's hat. The Louvre is scaffolded as the pyramid entrance is being constructed in the main courtyard of the museum. Will the glass pyramid be offensive? I think not.

Some things haven't changed at all and remain as I remember them. The Tuileries and Luxembourg Gardens are blooming, and children still play on the garden ponds with their colorful toy boats. The puppets at the Guignol still enchant children and adults alike.

The continuance of permanence amidst the buildings of antiquity such as the Place de Vosges, one of the oldest squares in Paris, brings me to a sense of permanence. I have a feeling of being a part of the continuum of history. Paris has cast her spell on me, and holds me in thrall. Once again she lives in memory until I return to the reality of her enduring charms.

A trip to London is also included in our European honeymoon

itinerary to Europe. Through the years, Connie and I continue to travel together and I have fond memories of our excursions.

The first house Connie and I purchase is a four bedroom home in the west side Ridgmar area of Fort Worth. Later, we purchase a large two story home in the historic Hillcrest neighborhood, part of the Arlington Heights area in Fort Worth. Connie and I enjoy almost 25 years of marriage together. Sadly, he passes away in 2008.

Today, I continue to live in the historic home in the Hillcrest neighborhood; the home has an abundance of space. I am blessed to have my granddaughter and her husband living in the larger section of the house. They are expecting a baby boy in March; my first great-grandchild! My children all live in the Fort Worth area.

As my octogenarian years pass, I begin to slow down in my activities. I am still active in The Woman's Club of Fort Worth with membership in The Shakespeare Club and the Beaux Arts Club. A few years ago, The Creative Writing Department published an anthology of the poetry and prose our members had written over the last decade. This anthology, entitled *Thanks for the Memories*, contains some of my short stories and articles. I attend church, enjoy luncheons with my friends, and celebrations with my family.

And, I am writing! Yes, here I am at ninety-one fulfilling the promise I made to the Ambassadors at the Chautauqua Institute so long ago. I am writing a memoir, A *String of Pearls*, describing my memories as a diplomatic brat in tow during the eventful years surrounding World War II: *Vignettes of a Diplomat's Daughter*.

The following is one of Chiquita's award-winning short stories, previously published in the anthology, *Thanks for the Memories*.

Ride!

Hang on! You're in for the ride of your life!

You're ready to go, but with much trepidation. The tunnel up ahead looks dark and intimidating. You have no idea what to expect. There is the sound of chatter and laughter behind you, so you decide to relax a smidgen when suddenly someone tells you it is your turn. Fear of the unknown grips you again as everything starts moving. Into the dark void you go. Your heart pounds and it seems like forever before you see the faint glimmer of light up ahead. Now what? Just because it is getting lighter, does that mean you'll like the ride any better?

Wow! What a light! You are momentarily blinded by a bright, almost florescent glow and can't make out a thing. As your eyes adjust, you gasp with pleasure. The sight before you is amazing! It is so bright inside the tunnel you can see every small detail as you look up ahead, as well as what you can see as you slowly pass by.

Now you have become a keen observer. Everything is bathed in soft pearlescent white intermingled with a lot of pastel colors. They are mostly pink and blue. Oh! Three transparent bubbles of varying sizes are coming right at you! What do you do? They float past you, unfelt. With a backward look you pursue them visually and then quickly turn to see a bright blue ball bearing down on you, followed by another, then another, then another. You feel them grazing by, but it is so gentle you barely notice. You are fascinated by the now varying shapes of blue which come after you, looking for all the world like a meteor shower. They are joined by white and pink bubbles. It is an incredible sight!

Whoops! You almost missed that! There in the wall to your right is a round indentation which looks like an overturned coffee cup. It is shallow, but with a distinctive ring round it, and it glows a pale peach color. The rim is touched by a blue tinge which casts a pale shadow within the half sphere. You pass it almost before you get to see it. But look, coming up ahead there is another one to your left. This time it is not quite so regular in outline, a little deeper, the edges a bit ragged, but it still beckons with its soft glow of white, peach and blue. You think of a marshmallow, or a cotton ball, only smoother, or maybe a baby's duvet cover – soft, soft, soft. It makes you want to crawl into it for a quick nap. No time! You have to move on.

Unexpectedly, up ahead, you see darkness and your heart gives a lurch of fear. You are not ready to leave this peaceful place where the ride seems leisurely. Besides, darkness always brings on anxiety, a feeling of insecurity. Why? You really don't know. You find yourself clutching the rail when all of a sudden you are once again bathed in pearlescent light and you realize you just turned a corner. Does that mean the light you have been seeing comes from you and not from some unknown location? You don't understand, but once again you see the fantastic softness and gentle glowing colors that make you relax and enjoy that which you are seeing. For the first time you notice a camel colored mushroom shaped column. Out of the corner of your eye you see something metallic snake out and immediately there is bright red everywhere. That too dissipates and the light colored atmosphere returns.

All of a sudden, you notice a roadblock just before you bang into it! You are once again clutching the rail and wondering what is going on. Slowly you have the feeling you are backing up and notice that everything you saw before has changed. Everything seems to have moved around. There are once more beautiful bubbles surrounding you – all the same lovely gentle pastel colors. You relax once more.

You hear a voice saying, "It's all over now and you did very well."

You realize what a privilege it has been to get a glimpse of God's creation. It has indeed been the ride of your life!

You have just read an account of an *Endoscopy* as viewed by the patient, doctor, and nurses.

Historical References

1. On 31 December 1992, Czechoslovakia <u>peacefully split</u> into the two sovereign states and today they are known as the two separate countries of the Czech Republic and Slovakia. When Chiquita lived in Prague in 1937 this central European country, created in 1918 when it declared its independence from Austria-Hungary after World War I, was simply known as Czechoslovakia.

2. After the invasion and surrender of Denmark in April 1940, Germany immediately invades Norway. In May Germany invades Belgium, the Netherlands, Luxembourg and France. French forces, supported by their British allies, initially make a determined stand, but are defeated by mid-June. France signs an armistice with the German forces on June 22, 1940. With the fall of France, Hitler's army conquers almost all of Europe. Italy joins on the side of Germany and the Axis Powers. A few countries like Spain and Portugal remain neutral and present no threat. Great Britain stands alone against the power of Nazi Germany. King George VI speaks to the people of Britain and the Empire in a radio broadcast. He tells them of the difficult times ahead and urges his people to "stand firm." Hitler offers Great Britain "a deal" he is sure they will accept. They decline. Their Prime Minister Winston Churchill believes that Great Britain is the only hope for Europe to ever be free of Nazi rule and vows that Great Britain will fight on.

3. Nicaragua, the largest country in Central America, aligned with the Allied Forces in the Second World War. Located just north of the Equator, it has a typically tropical climate with some variations between the seasons. It is much cooler in the mountains of northern Nicaragua where shady densely forested terrain and steady rains make the land ideal for growing coffee. The country produces some of the best coffee in the world.

4. Hungary entered the war in 1941 on the German side and suffered great losses in the ensuing years. By late 1944 Hungary was considering changing sides and entered into peace negotiations with the United States and the United Kingdom. Hostility with their former ally Germany resulted and Hungary was invaded by German and Romanian troops, the countries with which they had formerly fought. During the Christmas Season 1944, Stalin's Red Army forces approached and encircled Hungary, then fought their way into Budapest. For seven weeks the Red Army forces fought the German forces in what was known as the Siege of Budapest. Nearly 70,000 German and Hungarian soldiers, as well as almost a million civilians became trapped in the city. The fighting and bombing were fierce. Stalin ordered his troops to hold their ground at all costs. Hitler ordered his troops to fight to the last man. During the siege, tens of thousands of soldiers on both sides died. Nearly 40,000 citizens died as the result of military action, starvation, disease, and the mass execution of Jews by the far-right Hungarian nationalists. The city unconditionally surrendered to the Allied Forces in mid-February 1945.

5. May 8, 1945 marks the official end of World War II in Europe. Nazi Germany surrenders unconditionally to the Allies. Millions of people across the world celebrate Allied Victory in Europe. But VE Day does not bring an end to the Second World War. The War in the Pacific rages on and Japan appears to have the advantage. Allied

soldiers who fought their way across Europe are now waiting and preparing for transfers to the Pacific and Asia. A land invasion of Japan appears imminent.

6. In England, debutante balls, dating back to at least the 18th century, were originally intended as an avenue through which to present aristocratic young women eligible for marriage to prospective suitors of the same aristocratic class. These lavish events reached their peak of extravagance and popularity in the prosperous years of the 1920s. The London Season lasted for months with parties and dinners and dances. Beautiful dresses and elaborate presentation gowns of the era were created by the finest haute couture designers. The expenses of a London Season for a single debutante often cost a family the equivalent of one-hundred thousand dollars in today's economy. During the Second World War, these lavish affairs were discontinued. Postwar Britain struggled with severe rationing, massive bomb damage, rebuilding, and losses of fortunes. British society was becoming more egalitarian; societal barriers were fading. The feminist movement encouraged young ladies to seek careers and to go to college rather than seeking early marriage. After the Second World War presentations at court were revived by King George VI in 1947, but they were less exclusive and less glamorous than before the war. Young ladies no longer wore elaborate dresses, weeks of dances and parties ceased, and matrimony was no longer emphasized. In November 1957, Lord Chamberlain's Office announced there would be no more presentations after the following year's Season.

7. In the aftermath of World War II, Austria is divided into four occupation zones and jointly occupied by the United Kingdom, the Soviet Union, the United States, and France. The Red Army occupies only parts of Austria, including a sector of the capital city, Vienna.

About the Author

The effervescent Chiquita lives in Fort Worth surrounded by her extended family and many friends. She remains active in the Shakespeare Club and the Creative Writing Department of The Woman's Club of Fort Worth. A lifelong Episcopalian, she belongs to Christ the Redeemer Anglican Church of Fort Worth. Her home is filled with a myriad of antiques and memorabilia and her friends delight in having lunch among her many collections.

www.ingramcontent.com/pod-product-compliance
Lightning Source LLC
Chambersburg PA
CBHW040553010526
44110CB00054B/2663